THE KARATE EXPERIENCE
A Way of Life

THE KARATE EXPERIENCE
A Way of Life

by Randall G. Hassell

CHARLES E. TUTTLE COMPANY

Rutland, Vermont & Tokyo, Japan

REPRESENTATIVES

For Continental Europe:
BOXERBOOKS, INC., *Zurich*
For the British Isles:
PRENTICE-HALL INTERNATIONAL, INC., *London*
For Australasia:
BOOK WISE (AUSTRALIA) PTY. LTD.
104-108 Sussex Street, Sydney 2000

Published by the Charles E. Tuttle Company, Inc.
of Rutland, Vermont and Tokyo, Japan
with editorial offices at
Suido 1-chome, 2-6, Bunkyo-ku, Tokyo

2nd Printing — 1987

Printed in U.S.A.

This book is dedicated to
Harold, Alma, Esther, and Brian,
the four who have taught me the most.

Table of Contents

Acknowledgments

My deepest thanks and appreciation go to Dale F. Poertner, who provided invaluable assistance at every stage of development—from conception of the original idea through final preparation of the manuscript.

I also wish to express my thanks to my many students and friends, who have encouraged and supported me for longer than I can remember.

And special thanks goes to Charles O. Bauer II, who, although he was not involved in karate-do, taught me the essence of true inner strength. It is a debt which cannot be repaid.

Preface

The zen disciple, Inzan (1754-1817), one day went before his master, Gasan (1727-1797), to give an answer for his koan. Before Inzan could say anything, Gasan held out his hand and asked, "Why is this called a hand?" Before Inzan could answer, Gasan kicked out at him and asked, "Why is this called a leg?"

As Inzan opened his mouth to reply, Gasan clapped his hands and laughed loudly. So perplexed was Inzan by all of this that he bowed and silently left the room.

The next day Gasan said to him, "These are loose times for zen. The practitioners skip lightly over the koan, and they jump at all chances to write comments and poems. Everybody wants to be an 'expert,' but nobody is willing to submit to the proper discipline. No matter how times and people change, there is still only one way to obtain zen: You must put aside everything you have ever heard or done, and fill yourself with one purpose only. It is absolutely necessary to die and be reborn."

It is said that upon hearing those words, Inzan attained enlightenment.

—Traditional Story

As this is being written, most Americans are woefully unqualified to analyze and transmit the nature and essence of Japanese karate-do (the Way of the empty hand) to others. None of us has mastered the art, and those who have approached mastery have shown little inclination to give their views. After all, it is reasoned, we have many great Japanese masters, and they are doing a fine job. Who are we to be so bold as to attempt something the Japanese have not seen fit to do? Unfortunately, this reasoning disregards the whole of history. An art which originates in one culture can only be transmitted to another culture in a limited form by the originators. It has always been incumbent on the receiving culture to adapt the art to its own lifestyle. Without adaptation, the art will never reach and significantly influence the lives of the people. Without adaptation, the highest level an art can reach is that of curiosity, or perhaps sideshow. Perhaps the greatest danger inherent in analyzing karate-do as a way of life is that people will read the books and falsely perceive that the art is a game or system which, if the plan is followed, leads to measureable results. Such perceptions are patently absurd.

Nevertheless, karate-do deserves better than it gets in the West.

After nearly twenty years of pursuing and being pursued by this wonderful art, I have seen it relegated to exotic and vulgar displays in smoke-filled auditoriums, and I can no longer remain silent. Its reputation has been soiled and its fundamental methods are in grave peril in the hands of those who would confine the art to the recesses of boxing gyms.

No, karate is no longer a skill to be respected; and karate-do, the way of life, is all but unheard of. In America, karate is not even karate anymore. It is *kung fu, dim mak, jeet kune do, tae kwon do,* and a hundred other things, but it is not karate. For karate cannot be any of those things; it can only be karate, the Japanese art of "empty hands."

The point is that we are being hoodwinked. Karate-do does not—cannot—exist in the commercial world. It can only exist as energy in the minds and bodies of its practitioners. If karate-do is beneficial to human beings, it must be brought into focus in the mind's eye, analyzed, tested, and used.

Why karate-do? Because it has saved my life. As a companion, it has always pointed to the correct path, and it has never left me in doubt.

Karate-do is not a religion, nor does it border on the occult. And if we look to it for an answer, we are likely to find just another question.

The martial arts are like a hurricane, with all manner of refuse, good and bad, swirling in the wind. The eye of the hurricane is karate-do: not seen by those of us trying to avoid the storm, but nevertheless there. Real. Unperturbed. Calm.

This book is about the eye of the storm.

Chapter 1

Entering the Way

All two hundred eyes in the room were focused on the slight man wearing the white uniform and black belt. The room became still as he bowed and slowly raised his arms in a wide arc, crossing them in front of his chest and extending them outward to the sides of his body. The stillness was shattered by the heavy *thump* of his arms suddenly moving in and out, destroying imaginary opponents. The snap, snap, snap held us breathless, spellbound, as the young man moved quickly through a different time continuum—punching, kicking, slashing—returning to us with a fierce shout which vibrated the air even after his body had returned to its original, quiet position. For several seconds, we forgot to applaud, forgot to breathe. Then we came down, clapping, stamping, whistling and shouting. "What's his name?" someone yelled in my ear. "That," someone else shouted back, "is the great Kanazawa!"

I was stunned. Although I could not analyze it or explain it or describe it, I felt that something very important had just happened. I didn't know what it was, but whatever it was, it had jerked me away, for an instant, from my youthful righteousness and the street trauma of the hectic 1960's. Without reason or analysis, I wanted more. I wanted more of what I had seen, and I wanted to *be* what I had seen.

Hirokazu Kanazawa, then fifth degree black belt, was an All Japan Karate Champion who was making a world tour with his coach, Taiji Kase, and two other All Japan Champions, Enoeda and Shirai. They had come to the Midwest to show Americans what true karate was, and show us they did: Enoeda in self-defense against Shirai, the room quivering from the thunder of his powerful punches; Shirai driving Kanazawa backwards thirty feet with a furious flurry of kicks and punches, only to have Kanazawa leap high over the head of his opponent, kicking him in the back of the neck on the way down. The barrel-chested Kase watched all of it impassively until it was his turn; then he flattened all three of the champions as they attacked him simultaneously.

I had been studying various styles of karate since 1961, and was proud to wear my purple belt, symbol of the intermediate rankings below black belt. But on that day, my mountain of pride was reduced to dust. We would all have a chance to train under these Japanese masters, and while we were eager, we were also plainly scared. But rather than beat us up, what they taught us over the next three days was what the "basics" of karate were. We learned about stability and the value of the long, low front stance. We learned to grip the wooden floor with our toes and to snap our hips forcefully with each movement. Again and again, endlessly it seemed, we would punch and kick, kick and punch. Snap and tense, snap and tense. When we reached that infinitesimal instant when the mind numbed and the body could no longer move, Kase's gutteral scream would magically reach up to us from the earth and move our bodies against our wills. "Hai! Speed up!" Punch and kick, snap and tense, faster and faster we moved our limbs, our sweat-soaked uniforms crackling in the air like static electricity. At the count of ten, we all screamed from our stomachs, "Ei!" or "Osu!" Then silence, and awareness only of the sweat pouring off our faces and wetting the floor.

I had tried other styles of karate: the high, light movements of Shorin-ryu, the cat-like movements of Goju-ryu, and the acrobatic spins and jumps of Korean tae kwon do. Seeing the strength and beauty of this Shotokan style, I could not understand why everyone did not take it up. One of the masters explained, "The goal of martial art is perfection of human character, and many paths lead to the same goal. Because we have found the path which suits us does not mean that other paths are wrong."

The art of karate (literally, "empty hands") is a method of unarmed combat which was developed and systematized by the Okinawans after its introduction to the Ryukyu islands by the Chinese in about 1600 A.D. The Okinawans lived under severe military domination by the Japanese, and were forbidden to possess weapons. Under several successive Shogunates, the Okinawans were even forced to check out farming implements in the morning and return them before sundown. Since the Japanese warriors (*samurai*) were prone to attack Okinawan peasants on whim, the Okinawans were forced to rely on their wits and their bare hands for survival. They learned fighting techniques from Chinese seamen and gradually combined these with their own, indigenous techniques to form a system of combat which came to be known as *te* or *Okinawa-te* ("te" meaning "hands.") Over the centuries, Okinawa-te became highly developed, and tales of the exploits of its practitioners spread far into both China and Japan.

As Okinawa-te developed and gained more practitioners, it split into several distinctive styles (*ryu*), each reflecting the stylistic preferences of various masters in different villages. Several of these styles continued to be practiced as the Okinawan people gained their freedom and moved into the twentieth century. By 1905, the art was considered benign enough to be demonstrated in public. The first public exhibition was given by Gichin Funakoshi (1868-1957), a school teacher and poet who was widely known by his penname, "Shoto."

In 1917, Funakoshi travelled to Japan to demonstrate his art to a few Japanese, and returned to Japan again in 1922 at the official invitation of the Japanese Ministry of Education. The Okinawan masters chose Funakoshi to represent them in Japan primarily because of his fluency in the Japanese language. Further, Funakoshi was the best educated, most highly refined and cultured man among the Okinawan martial artists of that time. He was also the highly respected President of the Okinawan Martial Spirit Promotion Society.

Funakoshi was to formally introduce his art to the Japanese at their National Sports Exhibition, an annual event attended by the Royal Family. Being an extremely humble and sincere man, Funakoshi desired to represent all of Okinawan karate to the Japanese rather than just his own, favored style. Accordingly, he visited each Okinawan master of repute and asked each one to teach him the techniques which best represented the individual schools. These techniques he took to Japan in the form of fifteen *kata,* a kata being a formal exercise routine comprised of from fifteen to sixty-five techniques of blocking, punching, striking and kicking.

The art was already called karate by 1922, the ideogram for "kara" meaning "Chinese" and referring to the T'ang dynasty. Funakoshi never returned to Okinawa, and he later changed the character for "kara" to one drawn from the zen tradition, meaning "empty" or "rendering oneself empty." Thus it is that today when we say "karate," we are speaking of a purely Japanese art which conforms, in spirit and essence, to the traditional Japanese precepts of chivalry, duty, honor and so on.

There are many different karate *ryu* in Japan and Okinawa today, but the largest school by far is still Funakoshi's school—the Shotokan school. "Kan" means "building," and Shoto was Funakoshi's penname. Thus, Shotokan karate-do is "the way of the empty hand taught at Shoto's building."

Shortly before his death, Funakoshi lent his name to a new organization, the Japan Karate Association (JKA), and it is this organization which has produced the most technically proficient karate masters in the world. While the JKA has been maligned for its suspect and aloof political maneuvers, it undisputedly has led the way in internationalizing karate.

When I first put on a karate *gi* (uniform), Funakoshi had been dead less than four years, and the *dojos* (training halls) were filled with wondrous tales of the exploits of the old *sensei* (teacher). By the time I saw the young JKA masters in the mid-1960's, the old order was changing, giving way to the new. And, although I could not realize it then, I was changing, too.

Chapter 2

What is Karate?

The zen master Kaishu (1808-1878) was crossing a river one day in a boat with several pupils. It was raining violently, and the waves were tossing the boat to and fro. As the storm worsened, several of the young Buddhists became so frightened that they cried and shouted prayers to Avalokitesvara, the Buddhist goddess of love.

All the while, Kaishu sat calmly in meditation, breathing evenly and smiling faintly.

When the boat reached the shore, one of the pupils blurted out, "Sensei, weren't you scared?"

Said Kaishu, giggling, "A man is worthless if he can't take care of himself and let his *Do* sustain him in bad times. The goddess must be laughing herself silly at all of you."

—Traditional Story

The body of techniques and arts which has come to be known as Japanese martial arts (*budo*) is unique among man's organized physical activities. Martial arts are unique in that most of them purport to be sporting activities, but at the same time claim that sport is only a very small part of the overall discipline. Indeed, many martial arts such as *iaido* (art of the live blade) and *Aikido* (way of spirit harmony) have no sporting aspects at all. In most sports (hockey, baseball, football, etc.), the rule *is* the sport. Without official rules, there would be no hockey, no baseball, no football, and so on. We refer to such sports as "pure" sports because they are complete within themselves. They have no significant application to any sphere of existence larger than themselves.

For the most part, however, physical training in martial arts like karate consists of formalized methods for logically studying and practicing natural and necessary body movements; "natural" in that the movements are derived from intuitive response to surprise attack, and "necessary" in that the movements were borne of the survival instinct. All martial arts with sporting rules would continue to function quite well with the elimination of those rules. And all "pure" martial arts bear direct applications to the larger spheres of day-to-day life, personality, psychological stability and survival.

We say that Shotokan karate-do is pure budo because it conforms, in spirit and essence, to the traditional precepts of budo. The word "budo" is derived from Chinese characters which are combinations of other characters. "Bu" is a combination of two characters, one meaning "halberd" or "sword," and the other meaning "to stop." "Do" means way or path. Thus budo means "the way which promotes peace," or "to stop conflict." The philosophy of budo is opposed to armed conflict. In karate we strive to develop enough power to *control* any dangerous situation and thereby promote peace. And far more power is required to control a situation than simply to win a fight. This is similar to the "deterrent theory" of international politics: let the enemy know you have tremendous power, and he will be less likely to attack you. In budo, however, we do not menace or threaten the opponent, but simply control the situation on whatever level it develops. In this way, the opponent will get the idea quickly, and the cause of peace will be advanced. With these principles in mind, the informed practitioner will not view karate or other martial arts as sports.

In karate, the spirit of actual fighting (*jissen*) is thought of in terms of fire. There is nothing to fear from a fire which is contained and controlled; without fuel, it will soon burn itself out. The goal of the karateka under attack is to contain and control the attacker. It is rarely necessary to destroy him.

We call karate-do an art because it presupposes unique abilities in each human being, but does not encourage the development of these abilities for the purpose of competition with others. Karate-do seeks to maximize strengths and minimize weaknesses for the benefit of the individual alone. There is no game to win and no important match to lose. There is only the individual striving to bring his being into concert with the laws of nature and into harmony with the ebb and flow of humanity.

Basically, we may view karate on two levels: technique (physical) and art (spiritual). The Japanese possess a facility of language to differentiate between the two. They may say "karate-jitsu" when referring to physical technique only, or "karate-do" when referring to the total discipline of karate as a way of life. Do (pronounced as in "bread dough") is the Japanese transliteration of the Chinese "Tao," meaning "a way of life" or "the path to follow for a correct and fulfilling life." Jitsu is a generic term which means, simply, "techniques." The basic difference between Do and Jitsu may be thought of as the difference between a technical illustrator and a great artist. The illustrator is a technician who knows and performs the techniques necessary to produce his product. But the artist is one whose spirit and inner feeling guides his hand and allows him to create a great work of art. While most of us hold that only a select few possess this mysterious "inner force," it is the premise of karate that *everyone* possesses it and simply needs guidance and discipline to recognize and use it. The Japanese call this inner force *ki* (pronounced "key"), and purport that every living being possesses it to some degree. Perhaps it is best to describe ki in English as "energy." But it is not the kilowatt energy used to turn a turbine. It is the positive inner energy which enables an invalid to say, brightly, "I feel fine!" Negative (or lack of) ki is manifested in a laborer who consistently surpasses his co-workers in speed, efficiency, and production, but who always says, "I feel lousy." We may correctly discern from this that ki is strongly tied to personality and attitude, but it would be incorrect to assume that ki is spiritual in nature. Indeed, we would not necessarily say that a person full of positive ki is spiritual; we would say that he is "spiritful." Initially, this distinction may seem vague, but it becomes more clear as one progresses in the art. A great deal of confusion exists in the Western world over the nature of ki, and this is due to the prejudices of the Oriental writers who have tried to transmit the ki concept in English. Most written materials on ki have come to us from practitioners of Aikido, who are, by and large, very religious people. Most karate authors tend to ignore the concept, assuming that one who trains hard will come by it naturally. While the approach of karate masters is probably preferable, it is not adequate training for one who desires to lead others. Understanding ki lies in accepting that it is already there, that there is little one can do to "get" it, and that it will develop naturally through training and meditation.

The difficulty in describing ki to one who does not feel it is very much like trying to describe the odor of an onion. No attempts at description are adequate. The only way one can truly know the odor of an onion is to smell it, and the only way to know what ki is, is to experience it. In spite of the inadequacies of language to describe ki, it exists as surely as does the odor of an onion.

When we say that karate is a thing of the spirit, we mean spirit to be ki, with all of its attendant psychological attributes.

Chapter 3

Karate
and Physical Fitness

Today people in virtually every industrialized society are participating vigorously in various forms of physical fitness activities. This is particularly true in America, where the boom in tennis, racquetball, handball and jogging has been going on for several years, and shows no signs of abating. Large corporations are investing millions of dollars in the development of health and fitness facilities. And while increased concern for physical fitness is good for both the individual and society in general, it could be, through an art like karate-do, a whole lot more.

The benefits of karate training over other forms of exercise may best be seen from a historical perspective of physical education. While none of us was present at the dawn of mankind, we can assume that it was a very difficult time in which to live. As man struggled for survival against the elements and other creatures, he knew intuitively that the strong live longer than the weak. While this may not necessarily be true today, it was certainly true then. "Survival of the fittest" was a very cold reality. It is difficult and even absurd to envision a cave man doing push-ups and jogging, but we can readily accept that such men were, by our standards, inordinately strong. We know, for example, that primitive men often ran for miles, chasing an animal into exhaustion for the purpose of killing and eating it. And we know that while a horse is lucky to travel forty miles in one day, the Apache Indians in 19th century America frequently covered two or three times that distance on foot to avoid the U.S. Cavalry. When there were no machines to do the hard labor, muscle power was a very valuable commodity. The physical education of primitive man was not based on rules or organized sports; it was a natural by-product of his natural and necessary activities.

As man has progressed and industrialized, his reliance on fitness for survival has diminished drastically. Today we have machines to do everything. More machines and more technology require more education and intellectual development. While the level of literacy and higher education generally reflects the level of "civilization" of a society, it is also true that people in more primitive cultures today frequently outlive their "civilized" counterparts. Many factors in modern society contribute to this, of course, such as pollution of the environment, chemicals in the food chain, ever-mutating viruses, and so on. And while it is true that our life spans are longer than they were even five years ago, it is debatable how valuable and enjoyable those added years are in light of physical and mental debilitation. After many years of directing society along a path leading to more leisure time, people are beginning to place more emphasis on feeling good to better enjoy their leisure.

That regular vigorous exercise improves the overall functioning of the body is undisputed. However, there is no proof that people who exercise regularly live any longer, on the whole, than those who do not. We are not sure, for example, whether people who exercise regularly are healthier because of the exercise, or if healthier people tend to exercise more regularly than their less healthy peers.

Why, then, all the emphasis on fitness? Because people who exercise regularly *feel* a lot better than those who don't exercise, and their mental processes function more smoothly.

Virtually all forms of physical fitness today revolve around sport, not survival. While some people jog or do calisthenics daily with no thought of sport, they do so only out of a desire for fitness—not as part of an underlying philosophy. While sports share the philosophy of achieving excellence, that is as far as the philosophy goes. Achieving excellence in a given sport does not necessarily carry positive emotional, philosophical or mental factors into daily living. We have all seen champion athletes who become "stars" and prima donnas, using their inflated egos to intimidate others. At the same time, we know that becoming a champion at any sport is the result of long, hard work and sacrifice. What we may infer from this is that the hard work and discipline necessary to rise to the top in sports does not necessarily develop better character. Character development is presaged by understanding oneself and one's fellow man, but in sport it is necessary only to understand the opponent.

The karate view is that any physical fitness is better than none, but the best physical fitness is that which arises from the natural, instinctual processes which people inherit but have forgotten how to use. Such fitness comes from re-awakening and sharpening the natural impulse for survival. When survival is the key element, the matter of sport becomes inconsequential.

Thus while pop philosophies may evolve from sports (Lombardian thinking, for example) and the desire for fitness, it is better, we believe, for sports and fitness to evolve from an underlying philosophy. In karate we call this philosophy *bushido* (the way of the warrior), and we believe it develops the *whole* person—physically, mentally, emotionally, spiritually and socially. When sport becomes the main thrust of training, with emphasis on winning and losing, modesty and humility are destroyed, and the essence of bushido is lost.

Many karate masters say that karate is a natural skill, like swimming, which man has forgotten how to do; and, like swimming, karate will always be a part of the individual once it is awakened in him. This should not be taken to mean that once a certain level of skill is reached, we may stop training. Such an attitude, although common among Westerners, is very foolish. Any skill, including swimming, will be lost if not practiced regularly. A swimmer who does not practice regularly may well retain enough skill to save himself from drowning, but little else. Similarly, the advanced karateka who stops training may retain enough of his survival instinct to sense danger, but may be powerless to respond appropriately. And once the training stops, the body declines more rapidly. Again, it is most difficult to *enjoy* a longer life in a debilitated body.

Chapter 4

Karate

As A Point of View

A very rich man approached the zen master, Sengai, and asked him to write a poem or a prayer in praise of the continued wealth and affluence of his family

Sengai wrote, "Father dies, son dies, grandson dies."

Upon reading this, the rich man angrily flung the paper at Sengai and shouted, "I ask you for an heirloom and you treat it as a lark! What is this trifling nonsense?"

"I did not take your request lightly," replied Sengai. "You see, if your son dies before you do, you will be deeply grieved. And if your gandson dies first, both you and your son will feel grief beyond measure. But if your family, from generation to generation, dies in the order I have indicated, it will be following the true and natural course of life and death. *That* is true wealth."

—Traditional Story

Physically, karate is a method of unarmed self-defense, consisting of techniques of blocking, punching, striking and kicking. These techniques are designed for defense against surprise attacks from both armed and un-armed assailants. More than any other martial art, karate stresses defense against *surprise* attack, and since no weapons or special equipment are needed, it is the most practical of all the self-defense arts. Its only weapon is one's own body, a weapon which is always present. The training method is designed to increase awareness and sensitivity (ultimately eliminating the chance of surprise attack), and to develop tremendous force from small movements of the body.

Of greatest importance, however, is the fact that karate is a martial art which aspires to teach us a way of life. Central to this subject is an understanding of how differently the Oriental and Occidental minds perceive their world.

In general, the Western mind takes postulation and reasoning as its basic approach to viewing the world. Once a problem or unique situation is perceived, the relevant facts are gathered and analyzed, and a decision is made. That Western man has enjoyed a higher technology and higher standard of living, and has enjoyed them longer than the Orient, is undisputed. And growth in technology leads to more and more reliance on reasoning, logic and postulation (a phenomenon observed, for better or worse, more and more in modern Japan).

The basic Oriental point of view, on the other hand, is based largely on intuition or "gut feeling." This is perhaps due to lengthy societal development under more primitive conditions. For 2,000 years, Japan, for example, enjoyed a highly developed social structure without Western technology or a Rennaisance or an Age of Reason. The feudal system put weapons in the hands of an elite few, and the common people were forced by circumstance to devote their mental powers to basic survival. In the face of a sword, where immediate survival is paramount, there is simply no time for reasoning or postulating or thinking at all. Eastern religions developed accordingly, and were strongly influenced by zen after about 600 A.D.

It is this world view—intuition over postulation—which forms the foundation of Oriental martial arts, and makes them so difficult for Westerners to comprehend.

Further confusion is owed to the fact that the West views nature as an entity apart from man—something to be conquered, subjugated, controlled and changed. The East views man as an integral element of nature—an element which should exist in accord with natural laws. Western man fights against nature from the outside; Eastern man fights against himself to create a more pleasant existence from the inside.

The karate viewpoint is that what you see, or how you view the world, is what you believe. A Japanese legend illustrates this point:

It is said that a young Prince lived with his father in a palace on the shores of the ocean. The prince led an idyllic life and daily strolled along his private beach to gaze out over the water and watch the birds flying gently in the breeze. One day he was startled to suddenly see a large island appear with dragons and monsters cavorting and fighting all over it. As he jumped back, he was again startled by a voice behind him which roared, "What's the matter?" Turning, the frightened boy beheld a fierce looking man wearing a black evening coat with large sleeves.

"Who are you and where did that island and those monsters come from?" the Prince stammered.

"Why, I created them and put them there!" laughed the man.

"Then you must be God!" the Prince cried.

"Of course I'm God!" came the fierce reply.

Terrified, the prince ran home and blurted the whole story to his father.

"This man you saw," replied the father calmly, "Was he wearing a black evening coat with large sleeves?"

"Yes," answered the prince, "but what has that to do with anything?"

"The man you saw was not God," replied the father. "He was a magician. All magicians wear black evening coats with large sleeves. I am a magician, too, and he is my friend. Now, for the first time, you notice that I also wear such an evening coat. I asked my friend to create an illusion and frighten you so that you could become a man and see things as they really are. You have lived in illusion long enough. There is no island, there are no monsters, and you are not a prince. We are common people, and it is time for you to know that. I created illusions for your happiness as a child. Go and see for yourself."

After seeing that what his father had told him was indeed true, the boy returned home where his father was drinking tea with his friend.

"Father," said the boy, "You were right, but I cannot accept this. If I can't be a prince, I would rather be dead."

"Fine," replied the father, beckoning his son to kneel before him. "My friend will now kill you."

The boy thought it was a joke until he saw the very real blade of the friend's sword descending upon him.

"Wait!" he cried. "I understand!" Whereupon the three men wordlessly had a cup of tea and went out to tend their fields.

The karate view is that we are all like the prince, living with various illusions and believing them to be true. The purpose of karate-do is to help us see things as they really are, and to broaden the scope and depth of our understanding.

The essence of karate philosophy is the breaking of attachments. This is based on the premise that people naturally feel attachments to "things," and only a greater force will make them let go. This is easily illustrated by assuming you have $100 in your pocket. Until some greater force comes to bear, you will keep the money. The greater force which makes you release it may be a robbery, a bill to pay, or simply your desire to have something which costs $100. In any case, you remain attached to it, just as the prince remained attached to his illusion, until a greater force (in the prince's case, his impending death) makes you let go of it.

We live by memory and experience, and, like the prince facing death, we tend to fear and avoid things which are beyond our experience. Even with strong motivation, we naturally try to retain our attachments. Everyone wants to go to heaven, for example, but no one wants to die to get there.

The purpose of karate-do is to teach us to live fearlessly—not by memory, but in the present—without attachments to anything but life itself. Without illusion or attachment, we can live life like the Cherry Blossom: living brilliantly and filling a purpose, then letting go of life all at once when the purpose is fulfilled. This is called *isagi-yoku*: to let go of life when the time is right, without fear or regret or second thoughts.

Admittedly, this is not an easy course to follow, and

that is why karate is a lifetime art. The illusions and attachments are many and ever-changing, and constant discipline is required to overcome them.

Most Westerners will accept the premise that how you view the world determines what you believe, but then would use logic to follow with, "What you believe is what you do, and what you do is who you are." Thus when asked, "Who is John Smith?", we reply that he is a doctor, or a carwash attendant, or whatever. And we reply in that fashion because we perceive him to *be* what he *does*. The martial art idea is that "What you believe is what you are," and what you do may be irrelevant. We therefore may decide to be karate masters because we believe it to be paramount. At the same time, we may choose to do anything else (medicine, car washing, etc.) without giving up the broadening horizons of our minds. Again, the distinction is subtle, but necessary to achieve the ultimate goals of karate-do.

Chapter 5

The Ways of Enlightenment Go-no-sen and Satori

Matajuro Yagyu was born to a very famous samurai family of swordsmen. By the time he was in his twenties, it had become painfully clear that he had no talent for swordsmanship, and his father cast him out of the house.

In spite of his father's attitude, Matajuro knew that his father was very old and would soon need support and attention. Determined to gain his father's respect, Matajuro went to the famous swordsman, Banzo, and asked to be accepted as his pupil. Banzo watched Matajuro's kata and told him, "Your father is right; you have no talent at all."

"But if I really work hard at it," said Matajuro, "how long would it take me to be proficient?"

"It would take the rest of your life," answered Banzo, "no matter how long you lived."

"But suppose I become your dedicated servant and train every day. How long would it take then?" persisted Matajuro.

"Well, under those conditions, maybe you could make it in ten years," said Banzo.

"Good," said Matajuro, "but my father is very old, and I must become a master quickly, before he dies. How long will it take me if I train all day, every day?"

"Under those conditions," replied Banzo, "it would take at least thirty years."

"I don't understand this at all!" cried Matajuro. "First it's ten years, and now it's thirty years! I will do *anything* to become a master!"

"Alright," said Banzo, "but impatience is a great roadblock on the path to mastery. With your impatience, it will take you at least seventy-five years to master the art. I will accept you as a servant and student only if you can display patience and a calm and steady spirit."

Matajuro agreed, and he moved in with Banzo the next day. "You will live by two rules," Banzo told him, "and if you violate either one, you will be expelled instantly. First, you must do exactly what I say, no matter what you think of it. Second, you are forbidden to touch a sword or speak of swordsmanship."

For three years, Matajuro cleaned the master's house, made his bed, cooked meals, washed dishes, tended the garden and mended clothes. Then, one day while he was washing dishes and feeling sorry that he had ever entered Banzo's house, he received a terrible blow across the shoulders. Banzo had sneaked up behind him and whacked him with a wooden sword. The next day, Matajuro was tending the garden when Banzo jumped out of the bushes with a shout and whacked him hard on the back of the thighs. Day after day, and night after night, even when Matajuro was sleeping, Banzo attacked him unexpectedly. Eventually, Matajuro could think of nothing else. He still performed his mundane tasks, but his mind was filled only with the thought of Banzo's sword.

After a year of lumps and bruises, Matajuro became so

aware of his surroundings that he was able to evade Banzo's surprise attacks.

Shortly thereafter, Matajuro was universally
recognized as the greatest swordsman in Japan.

—Traditional Story

The fundamental methods of zen are passive, while the
fundamental methods of karate are active. In zen, the
process of enlightenment usually occurs over a long
period of time, which involves meditation, self-
deprivation, and daily guidance from the master. In
karate dojos, the word enlightenment is rarely, if ever,
heard. In the dojo, the training is always active. The
students are told to "move without thinking" and to
"clear the mind." But these instructions are always given
during physical activity, and are complemented by continuous emphasis on timing.

There are three basic strategies of timing in karate.
The first is called *sen*, which means seizing the initiative
or, simply, attacking. The second strategy of timing is
called *sen-no-sen*, which means waiting for the opponent's initiative and then responding. This is the
strategy of blocking an attack and counter-attacking.
The third strategy is called *go-no-sen*, which means that
one counters the opponent's initiative before it physically
occurs.

The ultimate timing we strive for in karate is, of
course, go-no-sen, so that we may counter-attack the opponent between the time his mind makes the decision to
attack and his body actually moves to attack. In self-
defense, go-no-sen enables us to perceive the attack
before it occurs, and thus never be surprised. When we

know an attack is imminent, we can usually escape without fighting. While the concept of go-no-sen may sound mysterious, it really is something anyone can learn through proper training of the mind, body and spirit.

The essence of go-no-sen lies in sensitivity to other people and, again using the analogy of the Cherry Blossom, "letting go" of attachment (in this case the attachment being thinking itself).

Thinking causes tension, and tension causes slow response. Even physically, speed is not a result of how quickly we contract the agonistic muscles, but how completely we *relax* the antagonistic muscles. In punching, for example, the main agonistic muscle is the triceps (the muscle which contracts to propel the arm), and the main antagonist is the biceps (the muscle which must relax to let the agonist do its work). No matter how hard we try, we cannot punch fast if the biceps is tense. Similarly, we cannot respond quickly if the mind is tense, and the more we *think* about an attack, the more tense the mind becomes.

If karate-do is "moving zen," and zen is the breaking of attachments to all things including thinking when we should be feeling intuitively, then karate-do consists of moving freely through intuition, with a clear mind unattached to fear, tension or anxiety.

Zen and Buddhism call this clear, intuitive state of mind *satori*, or enlightenment. Satori may be achieved in many ways—through meditation, devotion to arts such as tea ceremony (*chanoyu*), flower arranging (*ikebana*), paper folding (*origami*), and so on. But in karate we call enlightenment go-no-sen, because it gives us a distinct advantage over satori attained by other means: it gives us the ability, through strong techniques, to *take advantage of our perceptions* by counter-attacking when necessary. While a zen monk may perceive the attack before it comes, he may be powerless to do anything other than escape. While escape is always the preferred method of self-defense, it is not always possible. And karate techniques are for that once or never-in-a-lifetime when no escape is possible.

It is for that one attack from which there is no escape that we train with utter commitment and perform our techniques with *totality*—one hundred per cent effort of body and mind.

CENTERING

Hara is a term frequently used in advanced karate classes, and it means, literally, "center." "Move from hara," we frequently hear. Or, "You have lost your hara! Concentrate! Find your spirit!" While hara does mean center, it does not necessarily mean "center of the physical body," and herein lies some confusion.

The physical center of the body is the *tanden* or *seikatanden*, an area surrounding the body's center of gravity and ideally located on an imaginary line between the navel and the tailbone. When the instructor admonishes the student to tuck in his buttocks and abdomen, he is trying to make the student realize that the position of the center of gravity determines the body's balance. It should go without saying that poor balance always results in poor technique. Also important is the use of the large muscles of the hips and tanden for torque in developing linear and angular momentum. All body movements begin in the tanden because therein lie many of the largest, and potentially most powerful, muscles of the body.

Hara, on the other hand, implies "center of the being," or "center of the mind," or "central essence of feeling." Hara is that discrete force comprised of ki which makes our eyes show anger or joy or pity or grief. It is that unique property of mind which projects perception or confusion through the eyes. While the tanden is a specific part of the body, the hara should not be thought of in the same manner. It should not be thought of as lying in the abdomen or the head or the arms or the legs. It should be thought of as "feeling," full of energy, at once inside and outside the body. For example, if we are offended or angry and want to project that feeling to someone else, we can do so without verbalizing how we feel. Our attitude and demeanor make our feelings known. Without self-control, we do not keep strong emotions to ourselves, "bottled up" inside. When our feeling is projected to other people, it is no longer just inside us: it has spread to the outside, also. And this phenomenon is not limited to negative feelings; it is also manifested in love, joy, energy and so on. When we project our feelings to others, it is because the particular feeling is consuming the major part of our thoughts at that moment.

Hara implies that, through training and self-discipline, we are able to control our feelings and emotions and show them only when we want to. Even more than self-control, awareness of hara requires great concentration. If we can learn to concentrate fully on one thing and maintain that concentration under stress (attack), we will naturally develop great self-control.

Literally, hara refers to the stomach and abdomen and

the processes associated with them. In zen, the hara has two distinct points of reference for both physical and metaphysical functions. One is the solar plexus and one is the tanden. Physically, the solar plexus is a nerve center which controls the processes of digestion, absorption and elimination; the tanden is the ideal center of gravity.

From a metaphysical viewpoint, the bottom of the hara (the tanden) is the point at which the mind (ki) and body achieve equilibrium. When the mind and body are centered in the tanden, they radiate energy outward, in unison, like the spokes of a wheel or the petals of a lotus. By centering the mind and body in the tanden, we can overcome nervousness (hunched shoulders, stiff neck, aimless thoughts), and achieve deep relaxation. The more relaxed we are, the broader and more open will be our scope of vision, awareness and imagination.

In karate, we strive for go-no-sen, the clear, intuitive state of mind in which the body moves freely. We use hara to center our entire being—both physical and mental—on go-no-sen. And in hara we extend our feeling out to include ourselves, our opponent and the environment.

After years of training, we find that karate is a circle. What we strived for in the beginning (defense against surprise attacks), we return to after achieving the ultimate (go-no-sen), and the cycle repeats.

The cyclical nature of karate training is called *shu-ha-ri*. "Shu" means "learning from tradition," "ha" means "breaking the bonds of tradition," and "ri" means "transcendence."

While most of us remain in the "shu" stage for a lifetime, a few go on to complete mastery of physical technique, break away and try their own ideas, and ultimately transcend into the realm of a completely new technique or art. This is what Gichin Funakoshi did when he formalized karate and devised new kata for the Japanese. But Funakoshi found, as others have and will, that what lies beyond "ri" is "shu": the original challenge of how to make a stronger stance, a stronger punch, a better person.

Thus, the final answer to "What is karate?" lies not in the shiny new black belt of the shodan (first degree black belt), but in the worn and tattered black belt of the master—the belt which is gradually returning to white, fulfilling the circle.

Chapter 6

Zen and Bushido— The Great Empty Circle

One day as Dokuon, the great zen master, was idly smoking his long, bamboo pipe, he was approached by Tesshu, a famous samurai who was studying zen. Tesshu exclaimed ecstaticly that he had finally grasped the essence of true *kara*. He was finally empty, he said. The universe is empty, there is no difference between subjective and objective, and so on.

Expressionless, Dokuon listened quietly for a few minutes, and then suddenly smacked Tesshu sharply on the head with his pipe.

Enraged, the swordsman leaped to his feet and shouted, "You stupid old fool! That hurt! I could kill you for that!"

"My, my." said Dokuon calmly, "This emptiness is certainly quick to show anger, isn't it?"

Presently, Tesshu smiled sheepishly and crept away.

—Traditional Story

The word zen is a transliteration of the Chinese *chan-na*, which means "meditation." The concept of zen was brought to China from India by Bodhidharma, the first Buddhist patriarch to China, in about 600 A.D. Its

40

arrival in Japan dates to the end of the 12th century, which coincides with the emergence of the warrior class at the top of the Japanese feudal system.

Only in the West are "experts" so foolish as to delineate the intricacies of zen and tell us what it is. Indeed, the best description of zen lies in what it is not. Zen is not a doctrine, nor a metaphysical philosophy, nor a psychological "system," nor a religion. In the purest sense of the words, it has no rules, no ideology, no beliefs, no icons and no temples. Its masters are not bound by dogma, nor do they enter into monastic vows. If we believe them, we accept that zen offers no salvation and no condemnation. Zen does not proclaim a reward or a savior. At the same time, it makes no effort to deny us those beliefs as we see fit.

What zen purports is that a person's life is like a knotted rope, and that it is better to untie the knots one by one than to add more. The knots exist as illusions or appearances, and they obfuscate the original nature of the rope—straight and smooth. If zen has an ultimate goal, it is to see the essence of reality, to enter the "Void." But the Void of zen is the opposite of nothingness. It is at once full, complete and empty, like a great empty circle.

The spirit of zen defies logic, reason and analysis. It is, above all, direct awareness of reality through direct action. Zen rejects intellectualizing in favor of a flashbulb awareness of truth. A famous story illustrates this point:

It is said that Hakuin (1685-1768), a great zen master, was approached by an influential lord who asked him, "What is Heaven and what is Hell?"

Hakuin replied, "You scatterbrain! How could one as

stupid as you be a lord? Nobody in his right mind would obey such an ass!"

Infuriated, the lord drew his sword and chased Hakuin around the room, while Hakuin continued to shout insults. When the lord at last cornered the monk, he screamed, "I have you!" and raised his sword to strike.

"*That* is Hell!" cried Hakuin.

The lord hesitated, and Hakuin cried, "*That* is Heaven!"

The zen influence on Japanese culture commenced at the same time as the rise of the warrior class, and at first glance it seems paradoxical that zen, the philosophy of passivity, should be adopted by the fearsome samurai and their descendants. But the zen philosophy has two very appealing aspects for the serious fighter: 1) It calls for direct action without thought, and without looking back; 2) It proposes that the enlightened man is utterly indifferent to life and death. It was therefore natural for the samurai to pursue zen.

By the beginning of the 17th century, this pursuit led to a formal code of honor combining elements of zen, Buddhism, Shinto, and Confucianism. That code has come to be known as *bushido*, "the way of the warrior."

Bushido developed out of the very old Japanese tradition of *giri*, which means "duty" or "personal honor." As a feudal society, Japan was imbued with the idea that each class of society had a different *giri*, and the higher the class, the more rigid the *giri*. Since the samurai were at the top of the social structure, it was natural that their *giri* be the most demanding. And since the samurai were warriors, it was also natural that their code be concerned with matters of life and death. Since a fighter obviously will be better if he has no fear of death, the code of bushido developed with contempt of death as its central theme. For the samurai this was beneficial both in battle and in his social position. It made him the unchallenged guardian of the dignity of his class. That dignity consisted of loyalty, bravery, justice, integrity, benevolence and self-sacrifice. All of this he sought to maintain through direct action in a state of *mushin* ("no mind"). That is, what is done is done according to the code of honor, but without consciously thinking about it.

This state of mind is symbolized by the two statues who guard the gates of Japanese temples. One is Fudo, "the Immovable," and the other is Kwannon, "the God of 1,000 Arms." Symbolically, Fudo represents the fierce spirit of man, immovably rooted to the earth—fierce and unshakeable.

Kwannon, on the other hand, is the man with 1,000 arms—each working in coordination with the others—capable of performing all of the necessary tasks.

Fudo alone would not be a sufficient guard because he is so strongly rooted and fierce that he would turn everyone away. Kwannon alone would be so involved with his many activities that he would be apt to indiscriminately admit too many.

Together, Fudo and Kwannon represent the enlightened man—the man firmly rooted in his code of honor and being, but able to unflinchingly perform his everyday tasks and duties with perfect coordination, and without thought or worry.

The ultimate aim of true bushido is for the body to perform its tasks without the influence of the mind, and for the mind to hold fast to its foundations, regardless of what events surround or permeate the body.

Thus we may stand in even greater awe of the great karate masters who seem to retain and even increase their skills, in spite of advancing age and reduced training time. Their technical skill has become such an integral part of their being that it is completely divorced from any conscious efforts: Karate-do has become the man, and the man has become karate-do.

Chapter 7
Karate-do and Personality

It is correct to assume that if one spends a great deal of time at an activity designed to improve character, one will experience changes in personality. Gichin Funakoshi's most famous quote is, "The ultimate aim of karate-do lies not in victory or defeat, but in the perfection of the character of its participants." This, along with the principles of the dojo (to seek perfection of character; to be sincere and honest; to show strong spirit in all undertakings; to practice courtesy; to control bad temper), has come to be universally recognized as the essence of karate philosophy. But knowing just the essence of a thing does not imply total understanding. Indeed, in this case, like so many others, "a little knowledge can be a dangerous thing." It is especially important for instructors to delve more deeply into the meaning of character development as defined by bushido philosophy, so they may better guide their students. All people attaining the black belt ranking should also study the subject more carefully to better understand and assimilate the psychological changes they undergo at advanced levels.

Very little has been written in English on the subject of karate's influence on individual personality. This is due in part to the newness of the art in the Western world, and in part to the inability of Oriental masters to relate the depths of karate-do to Westerners in an acceptable fashion. While we are able to grasp the essence of budo

45

through training and meditation, the Japanese have no similar facility for grasping the essence of Western culture and thought without mastering all the nuances of the language.

The culture from which budo arose was and is largely contemplative, while American culture is largely utilitarian. It is not necessary to understand every detail or comprehend every fine nuance to benefit from zen or bushido. Clearly, it is far more difficult and exasperating for the contemplative man to absorb and assimilate the utilitarian minutiae, analyses and configurations of the West. Again, Western man wants all the details so he can subjugate nature; his Eastern counterpart wants to glide smoothly along with the flow of nature, irrespective of details. We are trapped, therefore, in the middle of a natural conflict between East and West. And whether or not the Japanese masters are willing to acknowledge the problem, they are trapped in the same space.

We undoubtedly lose a great deal by not mastering the Japanese language; but we all lose far more by the Japanese not mastering English. The attitudes and beliefs of any society or culture are deeply buried in the society's language.

Nevertheless, we can learn a great deal by studying the Japanese writings of the masters and applying their thoughts to our daily training. The meditations of two past masters speak most clearly to us on the subject of karate and personality. We choose the works of Jigoro Kano (1860-1938), the founder of judo, and Miyamoto Musashi (1584-1645), the "Sword Saint" of Japan. We select these two because their writings speak most clearly to both the layman and the adept, and because each placed great emphasis on the ability of men to benefit from the philosophy of budo in general, without limiting oneself to any particular art.

Kano, the great judo master, left us many volumes of writings. But in his last years, he distilled his thoughts on the value of budo into three basic precepts which have been handed down from generation to generation by his followers. They are:

1. *Jiko no kansei*—"To strive for perfection of character"
2. *Jita kyoe*—"Mutual welfare and benefit"
3. *Seiryoku zenryo*—"Maximum efficiency with minimum effort"

For Kano, budo was the basis of everything, but he recognized that each individual, even a great technical master, must consciously seek to make budo work for him, or he would gain nothing but physical strength. The foundation of Kano's philosophy was that strength in one area, such as becoming a karate champion, gives confidence and leads to success in other areas, *but only if we consciously seek success in those areas*. If we do not *consciously* seek to apply the principles of karate-do to our daily lives, we will not change at all. A foolish braggart who attains the rank of black belt is still, first and foremost, a foolish braggart, unless he consciously seeks to improve his character and personality through his training.

Of course, one who stays with karate training over a period of years will develop courage, self-control, discipline and awareness. But these are traits which may or may not accurately reflect the core personality of the individual.

We define the core personality as the abundance (or lack) of not just the traits mentioned above, but also health, intelligence, judgment and moral rectitude. Kano's maxim of *Jiko no kansei*—to strive for perfection of character—meant to strive in every area of life as if you were in the dojo. If something seems beyond your intelligence, approach it as you would a kata that you don't understand: break it down into pieces and methodically go over each piece again and again, until you master it completely. Seek guidance and help as necessary, but don't give up. When you face a problem requiring good judgment, approach it as you would an opponent who is about to strike. Try to catch the "feel" of the situation with your intuition, and then follow through boldly. Poor judgment is usually the result of thinking too much about consequences. When we dwell on the possible consequences, we are dwelling on matters beyond our experience. And we know that what is beyond our experience we tend to fear and avoid. The budo way, on the other hand, is to make the best possible decision *now* and complete the action without further thought. This comes from our training: thinking about the consequences of the opponent's attack or our response always results in defeat. For the samurai, it resulted in death.

Budo uniquely speaks to the matter of moral rectitude without moralizing. The precepts of discipline, courtesy, humility, respect and justice all relate to basic human morality without setting doctrinal rules which would cause damnation if broken. The keynote of morality in karate is justice. Gichin Funakoshi taught that the manifestation of a man's level of development in karate is seen in his commitment to justice. As we will later see in our study of Miyamoto Musashi, justice and injustice are considered to be part of the natural rhythm and timing of things. The pure heart which seeks to do the right thing in each situation is the heart of the true master. The morality of budo lies in the prevention of conflicts—all conflicts between human beings and conflicts within human beings. Budo literature is full of the concept that one whose heart and intentions are impure is defeated before he begins, but that one who is fully committed to justice will as readily go forward against 10,000 enemies as one if the cause is true. This thinking is supported by the fundamental zen attitude toward death. The true karate master will act without hesitation for the cause of justice, without regard to the possibility of death.

The second principle, *Jita kyoe,* or "mutual welfare and benefit," speaks to the matter of compassion. This principle is not different from the Christian principle of treating others as you would like them to treat you. What is important to bear in mind is that compassion proceeds from a position of strength, and its virtue lies in the *mutual* welfare and benefit of those involved. Senior karate people (*sempai*) are expected to fight with compassion against their juniors (*kohai*). But this is more than just moving lightly; it is a matter of both people benefitting from the exchange. And how does the sempai benefit from such an exchange? He benefits from consciously recognizing that what he is doing reflects every day life and from consciously studying the nature of compassion. By teaching, he also continuously re-learns the techniques.

Compassion always comes from a position of strength, but it is not true compassion if built on physical or material strength alone. The body weakens with age, and riches and positions may be lost. If one has not developed true compassion from a position of *inner* strength, he will receive no benefit when he needs it the most.

When we are young and strong, compassion is an easy matter. But, based on physical strength or position alone, it is not true compassion. In karate, we must strive not to be haughty or condescending, but always to place ourselves in the position of student, knowing little and seeking a great deal. In this way, we can develop our personality traits on the foundation of inner strength and true character, regardless of our position or physical strength.

It is important and instructive to note that a person who is truly strong and sincerely compassionate will be treated the same by people outside the dojo, who know nothing of his position in karate, as he is by his kohai and peers.

Kano's final, and most often quoted, principle is *Seiryoku zenryo*—"maximum efficiency with minimum effort." Anyone who has trained in karate for a year or two will instantly recognize the value of this principle in physical technique. In any physical activity, for that matter, it is best not to waste energy—to use only the energy and motion necessary to complete the task. In karate technique, the importance of relaxing and instantly summoning the energy and motion necessary to block and strike cannot be over-emphasized. Excess tension or thinking causes slow response, and results in inefficient techniques. This principle applies equally to daily life where decisions must be made regularly. Indecision, worry, confusion, frustration and guilt account for ninety per cent of the energy and effort most people put into life decisions. And none of those factors will change the net result once the decision is made. We all experience these feelings to one degree or another, and how we respond to such stress strongly influences our personality. The philosophy of karate-do is that the energy and effort spent on these emotions is far more than the minimum required, and results are far less than maximally efficient. It is better, we believe, to acknowledge the negative emotions, but not to waste energy on them. Using the best information at your command, make decisions boldly, with a clear, intuitive mind, and don't look back. If you later find, based on new information, that your decision should have been different, change the decision; but again, do it boldly.

This thinking is supported in whole by the long traditions of the martial arts: live fearlessly, live boldly, break attachments, die like the Cherry Blossom.

Our second writer for consideration, Miyamoto Musashi, was Japan's greatest swordsman ever, and is revered by the Japanese today as *Kensei* or "Sword Saint." Both the facts and legends of Musashi's life are well known to the Japanese people.

Musashi killed his first man in a duel at the age of thirteen, and was so invincible by the time he was twenty-eight that he discarded his swords and defeated his enemies with *bokken* (wood swords) or sometimes sticks. In at least one famous instance, he defeated a great master of the Shinto-ryu school of swordsmanship with a crude stick carved from the oar of a rowboat.

Unlike his contemporaries, Musashi lived through more than sixty duels and retired to die peacefully. In his later years, Musashi became Japan's premier swordsmith, sculptor, calligrapher, painter, and metal and woodworker. It was this amazing man who said that he came to understand the way of strategy (budo) at the age of fifty or so. He wrote, "Once you have attained the way of strategy, there will not be one thing that you cannot understand. You will see the way in everything." [1]

As perhaps the most famous man in Japan during his lifetime, Musashi consistently rejected riches and comforts. His humility was such that he spent the last two years of his life in a cave called "Reigendo." There he lived a life of quiet contemplation and wrote the *Go Rin No Sho*, the Book of Five Rings, finishing it just three days before his death.

We choose to study carefully the *Go Rin No Sho* because it is the master treatise of Japan's greatest warrior, the man around whom many of budo's legends and traditions revolve.

The *Go Rin* or five rings to which Musashi alludes are, according to Buddhist tradition, related to the five parts of the human body. Number one is the head, number two the left elbow, number three the right elbow, number four the left knee, and number five the right knee. These in turn, correspond to the Buddhist *Go Dai*, the five elements of the cosmos: ground, water, fire, wind and void. Accordingly, Musashi divides his text into five sections, each dealing with a separate cosmological element.

---

[1] *A Book of Five Rings*, Miyamoto Musashi, The Overlook Press, New York: 1974. (Translated by Victor Harris).

He prefaces the entire work with three, major precepts.

First, the essence of all budo is *kokoro*, which means "mind." Kokoro at once is comprised of and encompasses the heart, soul, mind and feeling (ki) of an individual, and is reflected in the individual's manners and demeanaor. Thus when we say in karate, "*Mizu no kokoro*" (a mind like water), or "*Tsuki no kokoro*" (a mind like the moon), we mean that the whole essence of the mind, heart, soul, spirit and feeling should be clear and reflective, like the surface of a pond, and see the whole environment like the moon, which shines down equally on everything before it.

The second great precept is that the strategy of budo must permeate our every action, both in the dojo and out, so that we may achieve *bunbu itchi*, "pen and sword in accord." That is, the firmness and steady spirit we gain in budo must be exhibited in everything else. The Japanese study the calligraphy of an individual and look for the crucial instant when the brush touches the paper to determine the state of his spirit and the level of his understanding. In karate, the most crucial instant occurs when the body moves from stillness to action, and from action to stillness. When the body moves, the breath goes out, and when the body stops, the breath comes in. It is between these two actions—the infinitesimal instant when the body is neither inhaling nor exhaling—that the spirit and centeredness of the individual can be tested. The mind is most steady when the body is full of breath; it falters and stops at the instant of change-over from exhale to inhale. This instant of falter is called *suki*, which means "relaxation" or, to the martial artist, "opening." Suki implies a space between two objects, the objects in this case being exhalation and inhalation. The goal in karate is to keep the mind steady, continuously.

In calligraphy the crucial instant occurs when the brush touches the paper, and it is called *raku-hitsu*. A single stroke of the brush (pen) tells the whole story of the writer's ki. Too much concentration at the beginning causes the stroke to trail off weakly; thinking about the end makes the beginning weak. Thinking about the beginning *and* the end makes the middle weak; and thinking about the whole stroke inevitably makes the stroke too large or too small. Only when the mind moves freely from hara, without thinking at all, can the entire stroke be made smoothly, with consistency, uniformity and proper proportion. We may, therefore, appear to move freely and smoothly in our art, but fail the test of the pen. Both are necessary; both must be the same.

Musashi tells us that the "Way" (Do) is in all things, and we cannot attain the Way if we remain ignorant. This further implies that there is no truth or understanding in the karateka who concentrates on physical technique only. The purpose of budo is to develop the *whole* person.

The third, and all-encompassing, point is the ultimate goal of "learning with no teacher." While we need a sensei to guide us, we must ultimately learn and understand by ourselves. No teacher can teach us how to feel, or how to have good judgment, or how to be moral, or how to be just. He can only guide us and give us exercises, physical and mental, to help us find our true nature.

Zen philosophy says that we will find and recognize our true nature when we can see our "original face" (*honrai no memmoku*)—the face we had before we were born and even before our parents were born. This implies that the vital life force, ki, is pure energy, and can be neither created nor destroyed. It may change shape or form or receptacle, but it is always what it originally was—energy. To see one's original face, one must look deeply inside himself and backward beyond his birth. In so doing, one finds that he fits nicely with the rest of the cosmos and that his emotions, desires and actions are illusions ingrained in him since he was born.

"Original face" is sometimes called 'original mind" (*honshin*), or "the true man" (*shinjin*), or "the mind of an infant" (*akago no kokoro*). By whatever name it is called, it implies an acute awakening of thinking (*kotsunen nenki*). It is a sudden realization of one's own identity, the realization of "one thought" (*ichinen*). It is as if another entity has come into being to direct one's actions, both in combat and in daily life. This psychological phenomenon is known as "no-ego" (*muga*). It is at this point that the man and his technique become one; the man is karate, and karate is the man. There is no distinction between the two, and the "original mind" guides the actions, unencumbered by the body or mind.

Musashi says that when we can see everything in a broad scope and understand how everything relates to everything else, then and only then can we find the Way. Later we will see that this includes studying small things and matters as if they were large, and large things and matters as if they were small, and from the juxtaposition of these opposites, come to know the truth.

It is interesting to note that while budo has employed this method of stimulating creativity and understanding for centuries, it is a concept not seriously considered by Western psychologists until the late 1970's. Now there is a growing body of scientists and doctors which believes that it may just be this juxtaposition of opposites which, more than any other single factor, triggers creativity in man. Modern science calls it "Janusian Thinking"; Buddhism calls it "Yin-Yang" or the duality of all things.

In the "Ground" book, Musashi talks of techniques and says that techniques are a "roadmap of the Way." [2] The key to this roadmap is timing. Timing is in everything, and there are different types of timing for different situations. Musashi says it is important to differentiate between active and passive timing (there is a time to move and a time to wait), fast timing for small things and slow timing for large things, distance and background timing (bring what you already know to the situation, and use your knowledge to perceive the right time to act), and off-speed timing (using timing the opponent does not expect).

We can easily accept that timing exists in all physical activities, but through budo we try to heighten our awareness and perception of timing and use it to our advantage not only in athletics, but in dancing, making music, sex and so on. The businessman can use timing in his dealings to influence gains and losses, and the employee can use timing to better manage workflow and responsibilities. Again, timing is in all things, whether we are aware of it or not. And this principle is not unique to Eastern thought, even though we are approaching it from the samurai point of view. The Judeo-Christian belief of

[2]Ibid.

"To everything there is a season" is in fact a very strong statement on timing.

While physical timing in karate may seem to be the most difficult to master, it is, if we follow Musashi's advice, the easiest. It is not sufficient to simply understand the timing of all things, but to *control* it. Musashi gives us nine broad principles, and says that if we master these, "you will be able to defeat ten men with your spirit." The principles are:[3]

1. Do not think dishonestly.
2. The Way is in training.
3. Become acquainted with every art.
4. Know the way of all professions.
5. Distinguish between gain and loss in worldly matters.
6. Develop intuitive judgment and understanding for everything.
7. Perceive those things which cannot be seen.
8. Pay attention even to trifles.
9. Do nothing which is of no use.

If these broad principles could be mastered, one could conceivably transcend all mortal problems and become super-human. Of course, they cannot be fully mastered, but at the same time every person could begin to live by these principles and improve daily. The key to budo is the *pursuit* of these principles along with pursuit of excellence in technique.

The "water" book speaks to the shaping of the spirit. Water is the symbolism because it always adopts the

---

[3]Ibid.

shape of its receptacle, and because it can flow at different speeds—sometimes as aere trickle and sometimes as a tidal wave. Further, water is clear, which implies clarity of mind and spirit. In the matter of shaping the spirit, Musashi lists twelve major points:[4]

1. Always maintain calm determination.
2. Meet each situation without tenseness, but not recklessly.
3. Keep your spirit settled and firm, but unbiased.
4. With the spirit calm, do not let the body relax.
5. With the body relaxed, do not let the spirit slacken.
6. Do not let your spirit be influenced by your body, and do not let your body be influenced by your spirit.
7. Do not lack spirit nor be over-spirited. Both are weak.
8. Do not let the enemy see your spirit.
9. If you are small in stature, know the spirit of a large opponent, and vice-versa; then do not be misled by the reactions of your body.
10. With an open and unconstricted spirit, look at things from a high point of view.
11. Cultivate your wisdom and spirit: learn public justice, distinguish between good and evil, study the ways of other arts one by one. When you cannot be deceived by men, you will have realized the wisdom of strategy.
12. Learn from battle to develop a steady spirit.

[4]Ibid.

Again, these are not principles which will be mastered tomorrow or next week or next month or next year. Perhaps we may never truly master them, but the point of budo is to *try*.

Also in the Water book, Musashi describes the methods of using stance, gaze and arm position for cultivating the spirit. The point again is that the spirit is like water and adopts the shape of its receptacle, the body. It is important to note that Musashi was describing sword fighting, but his principles of stance, gaze and arm position are virtually identical to those taught in modern Shotokan karate:

Principles of Correct Fighting Stance
1. Head erect.
2. Forehead and bridge of nose unwrinkled.
3. Narrow eyes.
4. Slightly flared nostrils.
5. Hold the line of rear of neck straight. Instill vigor from the hairline down through the body.
6. Shoulders low.
7. Buttocks tucked in.
8. Strength in lower legs.
9. Brace the abdomen against your belt and do not bend at the hips.
10. Maintain combat stance in everyday living.

Principles of the Twofold Gaze
1. Gaze should be large and broad.
2. Perception is strong; sight is weak.
3. See distant things as if close, and close things as if distant.

4. Do not be distracted by insignificant movements.
5. See (perceive) to both sides without moving the eyeballs.

Principles of Positioning the Arms
(The Five Attitudes)
1. Upper (*Jodan*)
2. Middle (*Chudan*)
3. Lower (*Gedan*)
4. Right Side (*Migi*)
5. Left Side (*Hidari*)
   (Of these, the middle is the most preferred and effective.)

Musashi uses "Fire" as the symbolism for actual fighting (*jissen*), because the spirit of actual combat must be fierce and burning. The underlying principle of actual combat, however, is to train day and night, under all conditions, ill or well, so that your spirit will remain the same, regardless of the surrounding conditions. In the Fire book, we read of the strategy of fighting (sen, sen-no-sen, go-no-sen) and how to use the *kiai* (a loud shout from the pit of the stomach) to get into the rhythm of the situation. But all of this amounts to nothing without a fierce, burning spirit.

The "Wind" book is comprised of practical advice about acquainting oneself with the techniques and training methods of other schools and styles. This study is not undertaken to learn how to defeat other martial artists, but rather to broaden one's scope and to find superior training methods.

Finally, the book of the "Void" is presented as having no beginning and no end. The Japanese character for the Void is the same character used for the *kara* of karate, and comes from the zen principle of "rendering oneself empty." This means empty of illusions, false pride, false confidence, and intellectual committments to psychological "systems" and "methods," all of which obfuscate the true nature of man. To live in the Void is to live in tune with the laws of nature and to respond to *any* situation accordingly. To live in the Void is to know intuitively the natural rhythm of the situation and to strike naturally.

The Void is an expression of true karate: moving freely through intuition, with a clear mind unattached to fear, tension or anxiety. We are born in the Void, and we die in the Void.

When we say that we practice our techniques until they become "second nature," we are also saying that we practice budo until we find our "true nature." When we can reach the intuitive state in which we learn our true nature (learning with no teacher), Musashi says, "Then you will come to think of things in a wide sense, and taking the *Void* as the *Way*, you will see the *Way* (*Do*) as *Void* (*Kara*)." [5]

What we hope all of this will bring us to is a state called *myo* in Japanese. *Myo* is a creative and original force emanating from the unconscious, or from the "original mind." *Myo* is the state of the true master who moves creatively and spontaneously from his unconscious, irrespective of technique or skill or universal

[5]Ibid.

concepts. It is the state of the spider spinning its web, the bee building its hive, the cool breeze blowing softly across the dew at dawn.

Myo is attained when the conscious mind delves deeply into the unconscious and perceives the Void as all things and nothing. In *myo*, the true nature of things is realized, and the lines between physical, psychological and metaphysical are forever destroyed.

Such is the nature of *kara*; such is the nature of *Do*.

Chapter 8

Stress and Anxiety

The zen master Tokai was sleeping one night when a fire broke out in the kitchen of the temple. A pupil rushed into Tokai's room, screaming, "Fire, sensei! Fire!"

"Fire?" said Tokai. "Where?"

"In the kitchen, sensei! You must get up! The monks are trying to put it out!"

"Well," said Tokai, yawning, "the kitchen is on the other side of the temple. If the fire reaches my hallway, you be sure and wake me up again, okay? Goodnight."

So saying, Tokai lay down and slept soundly.

—Traditional Story

It may be that stress and anxiety are the most deadly enemies of modern man. Before one can attain the deeper levels of karate-do, he must understand the nature of stress and anxiety, and strive to calm the mind.

Just as strong emotions like joy and sorrow always manifest themselves in some part of our lives, anxiety will also manifest itself, in one form or another, in our bodies. Different people react differently to stress. Some develop ulcers, some skin problems, some heart trouble. The stress itself is the outer force which bears down on us and causes anxiety. Anxiety, in turn, plays a strong role in pain, allergies, obesity, learning disorders, speech disorders, sexual maladjustment and mental illness.

Anxiety is a very unpleasant state of tension or uneasiness which arises from the mind's perception of stress as a danger to the body. When we fight against anxiety, we often over-react, and cause both the body and mind to develop symptoms which indicate that a severe conflict is taking place. These symptoms often develop into neurotic and non-organic illnesses. This occurs because the body is well-equipped to respond to fear, fear being a reaction to a short-lived, external threat or danger. But the body is ill-equipped to maintain the fear response over an extended period of time. Fear occurs in response to a specific stimulus, while anxiety is like a "drawn out" fear of something we cannot see or recognize or specifically define. When the brain perceives a threat, it "super-charges" the body's defense mechanisms and temporarily suspends a number of normal body functions. In fear, the heart beats faster, the blood pressure rises, and blood is redirected from the stomach and intestines to the heart. The spleen contracts and discharges its supply of red blood corpuscles to provide the increased oxygen necessary for the extra energy needed for fighting the danger. And the mind automatically decides to either escape from the danger or fight it. This is universally known as the "fight or flight" syndrome.

In anxiety, these functions tend to occur on a more continuous basis, and the body inevitably suffers. Physical manifestations of anxiety frequently include extreme muscle tension, greatly increased energy expenditure, fatigue, fast pulse, high blood pressure, nausea, heartburn, aberrant digestion and elimination, and many others.

When we understand the potentially devastating effects

of anxiety, we have no trouble deciding that anxiety is a feeling we do not want. Through the practice and study of karate-do, we can find release from anxiety, and lead productive, vigorous lives, regardless of stress.

The basic karate method of achieving emotional strength and overcoming anxiety involves strenuous training of the body and mind together

Karate is, above all, a physical, dynamic athletic endeavor. Only through hard training can the body and mind be brought into unison. All of the passive arts such as yoga and transcendental meditation have their benefits. But they are not enough to preserve our lives in time of danger. In karate, we can realize our own nature, clear our minds, and at the same time learn to protect our precious lives from destructive forces. It is not enough for one to simply meditate on the nature of the universe and his surroundings; he must be concerned with the precious nature of his body and the life within it. Karate can help in this respect. It may be difficult at first to correlate the ideas of gentleness, non-resistance, and courtesy with the medium of breaking bones, but that is where karate is, and it is where we must strive to be, also.

Even if we fully understand the nature of stress and anxiety, and even if we come to a piercing awareness of how to overcome them, we will not have gained much if we lose our lives to a mugger. No matter how much peace of mind an individual may gain through meditation, he will have great problems when confronted with a violent attack. Direct attack is the most stressful situation possible for any person. And how we react at such times is a measure of our inner strength and our level of understanding.

What must be done is for the individual to face stress and anxiety in the controlled atmosphere of the dojo, and learn first-hand what it is all about.

Karate is primarily a self-defense art, and as such, its method is to place the practitioner in one stressful situation after another and teach him to cope. In the early days of karate development, the students were not students in the purest sense of the word. They were men whose lives were in danger and who were interested in preserving their lives and the lives of their families and friends. Each encounter was a life and death struggle. Punches and kicks were not practiced to win a tournament or to look pretty, but were practiced with the idea that not doing them correctly would cause the student to lose his life. With this in mind, it is somewhat easier to understand why the old masters are still held in awe today. We sometimes think they were so proficient because they invented the movements. The truth is that they were more proficient than we because they were struggling for their lives.

In the dojo today, we do not think much about life and death when we train, and this is unfortunate. For it is in the life-death struggle that karate has its roots. The training must therefore be strict, disciplined, and at times severe.

Training in sparring and kata must be conducted with the utmost stress and committment. The instructor must push his students physically to levels which they thought they could not attain. In sparring, all attention must be directed to the life-death struggle, and the training must be deadly serious. This is not to say that anyone should be hurt, but it is very important for advanced students to at least occasionally feel that their personal well-being is in danger, and that they can alleviate the danger by doing their techniques better, stronger and more consistently. It is the job of the instructor to instill in his students this feeling of seriousness.

Basically, the task is accomplished in the dojo by placing the student in a strenuous, stressful situation in which he places his trust in the instructor, and seeks to overcome the stress by trying harder. Basic sparring should not be done simply for the perfection of physical technique; rather, it should be done in such earnest and with such intensity that the student actually feels tense. When the correct block and counter-attack is performed in basic sparring, the student should feel a great relief and a sense of accomplishment.

The more advanced a student becomes, the more often he should be pushed by the instructor toward his physical limits. For the student who perseveres, the limits will constantly expand. He will find, in time, that what troubled and exhausted him six months earlier is no longer a problem. He must be forced to feel danger and exhaustion, but he must not be allowed to become discouraged. Thus, each class should end on a positive note. If the students have been pushed very hard, they should be allowed to finish the class with something positive.

This fundamental karate training method is analogous to Aristotelian tragedy: the students must experience fear and anxiety, be allowed to overcome it in a controlled environment, and experience the feeling of relief which leads to confidence and emotional strength.

In this regard, it is the task of the instructor to push his students hard. He must show compassion, but must realize that his main task is the development of strength and confidence in his students. Anything less than rigorous training cheats the students and gives them a false sense of confidence which may put them in danger later. The sincere student must trust his instructor and realize that the instructor is severe not out of hatefulness, but out of his respect for the nature of life and his desire for the student to learn how to protect it.

Karate training is not without its ups and downs and pains. But karate-do is a very valuable thing for human beings to seek, and anything so valuable cannot be attained without extreme effort. As in all athletics, pain is a recurring fact of life. If the athlete never experiences pain, he will never have the courage or will power to excel. While there are very few serious injuries in karate, there are many, many bruises, strains and abrasions. This is a natural part of any athletic activity, and should be used as a tool in the development of the inner spirit of the individual. While pain should not be taken lightly, it should be remembered that most people are only in as much pain as they allow themselves to be. That is, in the case of minor pain, it is more our anxious reaction to the pain than the pain itself which causes us to be uncomfortable. All injuries should be treated properly, but the student must not allow himself to become wrapped up in how badly something hurts. The student must empty his mind of minor pain, and call forth his ki to heal the injury and sustain him through training. After all, should we not be aware that we might be attacked when we are in pain? And if we continually coddle ourselves in the dojo, will we not be in drastic straits if someone attacks us and we react to the pain rather than the attack? The point is that most pain is minor, temporary, and can be overcome by concentrating on something else. Recuperative therapy in hospitals following surgery dictates that the patient be forced to move about, that he be kept active, so that he will not lay in bed thinking about his pain, allowing his body to degenerate.

The more the mind is occupied with other things, the less response there is to pain.

Chapter 9

Training the Mind

In about his 75th year, the zen master, Goyu (1834-1915), was told by his doctor that he needed surgery on his eye. Goyu told the doctor to do what must be done.

Anesthesia was not a highly developed science at that time, and was usually reserved for the very old, to help them stand the pain. On the day of the operation, the doctor explained the anesthesia to Goyu, who said, "I do not need that; just do what must be done."

Throughout the operation, Goyu sat calmly, un-flinching, in a straight-backed chair.

The doctor said it appeared as if Goyu were somewhere else.

—Traditional Story

Essentially, psychological well-being is strived for in karate through harmonizing the functions of the body with those of the mind. This is accomplished through arduous physical training with strong emphasis on discipline.

A conscientious instructor will lead his students along the physical path without a great deal of technical emphasis. He will encourage the student to "feel" the essence of each technique in his mind and body. As the student progresses, more technical data may be added. But care must be taken to keep an even balance between doing and theorizing. Too much emphasis on either results in the decline of the other.

No one can truly understand the essence of karate through physical training only. Conversely, no one can realize the truth of karate simply by meditating. The mind and body must function as one, and they must go through the process together.

Students of the art may best achieve their goals if they concentrate on certain basic ideas, and try to relate them to their body movements.

Following are the most commonly emphasized concepts in the dojo.

A MIND LIKE WATER

Consider the water in a pond or forest lake. If the water is calm and clear, it will reflect everything around it, like a finely polished mirror. If the water is in tumult, the reflections will be distorted.

In karate training, we should strive to imagine our minds as the calm surface of that pond, seeing everything around us, exactly as everything is. As the pond reflects everything around its entire circumference, so should our minds try to reflect everything in a circle around us. In this way, the mind can clearly perceive everything that is relevant in the external environment—even the most minute movements of one's opponent.

If any thought is allowed to enter the mind, the effect will be that of casting a stone in the water. The clear surface will be distorted, the reflections altered. The movements of the opponent will not be clear, and the proper response will be left to chance.

A Mind Like the Valley

A quiet valley will carry even the smallest sound from end to end.

In a similar fashion, a quiet and peaceful mind will hear every sound of an opponent, and will hear it without distortion. A rush of thoughts or feelings of fear will enter the valley of the mind like a howling wind, changing our perception of the sound and its location. Strong fear is like a tornado, blotting out the sound of an opponent completely, causing certain defeat.

One must ignore the wind and engage the opponent, or fight the wind and lose sight of the opponent.

Thus, we must try to put our clear pond in the valley of the mind, seeing and hearing clearly.

A Mind Like the Moon

Overlooking the clear pond in the valley of the mind should be the moon.

The light of the moon is different from the light of the sun. While the sun shines brightly and casts harsh shadows, the moon shines more evenly and gently. Harsh shadows conceal, while softer shadows do not hide completely. Further, the moon shines down equally on all before it, without the sharp angles of the sun.

A mind like the moon in karate means that one should see his opponent's whole body as equally as possible. Seeing only one part of the opponent's body will cause one to lose sight of the rest, and defeat is inevitable.

The moon, then, shines on the pond in the quiet valley of the mind, and we become aware of all that is around us.

In a state of *myo*, the mind should not perceive the difference between the moon in the pond and the moon in the sky. The demarcation between subjective and objective is erased, and the defender becomes one with the attacker.

ONE PURPOSE

Of the many stories of warriors in feudal Japan, the following is frequently passed from karate instructors to their students to describe the state of the empty mind.

It is said that a young monk inadvertantly insulted a great samurai. Although the monk could not understand what he had done wrong, he immediately sought to apologize. The samurai, being a braggart and one full of self-pride, rejected the apology and demanded satisfaction. No matter how hard he tried, the monk could not dissuade the warrior from his foolish position. Being of a lower caste in society, the monk was obliged to obey the ruffian's demands, and agreed to meet him at dawn for a duel to the death. As was the custom, the warrior gave the monk a sword and sent him away to prepare for the battle.

The monk, having no knowledge of swordsmanship or fighting, was sure that he would lose his life, and went to the master of his monastery for advice.

"Your mind is too full of fear and thoughts about what will happen," said the priest. "Sit in solitary meditation all night, with the sword raised above your head, as if prepared to strike. Close your eyes and meditate only on the sensation of 'cool'. When blade meets flesh, the sensation is one of thin and cool. Clear your mind completely.

Empty it and then fill it with one purpose only: When you feel something cool, strike down with the sword."

Though perplexed at first, the monk obeyed his master. Throughout the night he held the sword above his head and meditated on the one thought only, until everything else left his mind.

When he met the loudmouth the next morning, he bowed, raised the sword above his head and closed his eyes. His fear was gone, and he waited to feel the sensation of cool steel.

"Fight, coward!" cried the samurai. "Open your eyes and fight!"

But the monk made no response. He heard nothing and saw nothing. His only purpose was to make his one strike.

It is said that the samurai, after a long period of intense silence, sheathed his sword, bowed humbly in defeat, and walked away.

What the samurai perceived was what we must try to show our opponents in karate and in our daily lives: a tranquil mind, so filled with one purpose that the opponent cannot win.

It is impossible to attack emptiness.

BREATHING

In karate, as in other martial arts, breathing methods are very important tools in the development of awareness and a tranquil mind. Being a continuous, natural activity, breathing is a tool which we can use anywhere, anytime.

The zen tradition has always associated breathing with the spirit, and all martial artists are aware of the importance of proper breathing in controlling their bodies. In karate, breathing is considered in relation to two types of body action—active and passive. On the active side, the control of breathing may be considered an integral part of the athletic activity. Proper breathing, coordinated with body movements, manifests itself on the active side as endurance. On the passive side, breathing methods are used to enhance the coordination between the mind and body. It is suggested that all martial artists regularly practice the following exercises.

SITTING

1.   Kneel on the floor, crossing your feet at the insteps. In the beginning, it may be more comfortable to kneel on a soft surface such as a mat or folded blanket. Keep your back straight, and rest your buttocks as lightly as possible on your heels. This position usually feels uncomfortable at first, and may require some exercises to stretch and loosen the ankles and knees. Relax your shoulders and rest your palms on your thighs. The most important point is to remain relaxed while keeping your back straight and your chin tucked in. If you find it utterly impossible to kneel properly, then sit in cross-legged fashion. But it is important that you continue to try to assume the *seiza*, "formal kneeling position."

2.   Begin by closing your eyes and forcefully breathing out all the air in your body, through your lips. As you exhale, make a faint "ah" sound. When you feel that you have exhaled completely, try to exhale some more. As you breathe out, let your body incline forward slightly.

3.   As soon as you have exhaled completely, start breathing in *slowly*, through your nose. Think only about

controlling your breathing action. As you inhale, imagine that the air is going up, into the back of your head, rather than to your lungs. As the air comes in, let it pull your body erect, stretching your neck and back upwards, in a straight line. When you can inhale no more, drop the air in your head down through the body, to the lower abdomen. *Note:* A) Drop the air *slowly,* like a large boulder rolling down a hill. B) Keep the buttocks and rectum *taut*, as if to prevent the air from escaping, but *do not tense the stomach*; remain relaxed.

4. Hold the air in your abdomen and concentrate on nothing else. Holding the air for ten seconds is good for a beginner, but each day you should try to hold it a little longer. After two weeks of practice, you should be able to hold the air and concentrate on it for thirty seconds. After two months, you should be holding it for at least one minute. Remember to hold the air in your abdomen without tensing; do not let it rise and cause your chest and shoulders to tense. Also, if you find that you are having difficulty holding the air in for the time prescribed here, do not lose hope. The times mentioned above are merely general guidelines. It is far more important to breathe comfortably and concentrate on the breathing.

5. Exhale the air through your mouth, very slowly, with a faint "ah" sound, and repeat the exercise.

The effects of this type of breathing are numerous. The psychological benefits will be noted after a few weeks. Your powers of concentration will increase, and you will feel more at ease. If you feel uncomfortable doing the exercise, (and you will), force your attention to the control of your breath. Count your breaths on the exhale, but do your utmost to keep your attention focused fully on your breathing. In time, you will be able to concentrate fully on your breathing, and you will feel no pain or discomfort in your legs. This exercise is a tool for strengthening the will and coordinating the mind with the body.

Physically, deep breathing more fully oxygenates the blood stream and often has an euphoric effect. It also aerates the lower one-third of the lungs, which is where many lung diseases begin.

Repeated practice of this exercise will result in a strengthening of will and concentration, plus generally better respiration.

THE TANDEN

The tanden is the lower stomach, having a center located in the middle of a line between the cocyx and the navel. The tanden is the most important part of the body in the performance of karate techniques, because it is the ideal center of gravity for the body. Philosophically, the tanden is believed to be the spirit center of the human being. Therefore, all physical movements begin in the tanden, and all breathing is concentrated in this region. On a physical basis alone, it is good to concentrate on the lower abdomen.

When performing the breathing exercises, it is good to use imagination. When you inhale to the back of your head, imagine that the air is mixing with your thoughts and bad feelings. Then drop these feelings and thoughts down to the tanden with the air, forcing the good parts into the blood stream. When you exhale, imagine that you are sending your bad thoughts and feelings out to the ends of infinity.

If the approach seems sophomoric at first, remember

that the difficulty in karate lies in its simplicity. It is so natural that we often overlook it. But once attained, the beauty of karate-do will never be lost.

When to Meditate

The breathing method described above is a slight variation of standard zazen meditation. Any activity which causes the individual to realize his own "inner self" may be thought of as meditation. In karate, we refer to this meditative exercise as *mokuso* (quiet contemplation), and it has nothing to do with religion. The mokuso exercise is performed for about one minute before and after each class in the dojo. Before the class, the student tries to mix his thoughts with air and clear his mind in preparation for study. Following the class, he again clears his mind in preparation for return to his daily life.

It is essential that mokuso be performed before and after training. For the person who wishes to truly understand himself and his art, it is suggested that the exercise be performed every day for one to five minutes, just before retiring and immediately upon rising. If one will persevere in this regard, he will realize immeasureable benefits in the form of alertness, better digestion and respiration, and increased powers of concentration.

Other Methods

When one has performed mokuso for about a month, he should try the same breathing exercises with the body in different positions.

Try lying on your back, without a pillow, arms at your

sides. When you breathe in, imagine the air going down to your heels, following the contour of your back.

Try mokuso sitting in a chair, and try it walking.

The ultimate aim, of course, is to be able to maintain mokuso at all times, and to eliminate the *suki*—the space between exhale and inhale.

That is why karate is often referred to as "moving zen." It is an art which requires us to have a calm mind in the midst of turmoil, regardless of the circumstances.

Realizing the empty mind of karate-do is the feeling of escaping into the eye of a hurricane—a feeling of safety and release from fear. But sitting in the eye of a hurricane is dangerous: the whirlwind continues to move, and will recapture the immobile person. Only one who continues to move can remain safe. The student who perseveres will be rewarded. Karate will become the man; the man will become the eye of the storm.

Chapter 10

Samurai Strategy

Tsukahara Bokuden (1490-1572), one of Japan's greatest swordsmen, wanted to test the abilities of his three sons, all of whom he had trained in the way of the samurai. To do this, Bokuden placed a pillow over the curtain on the door to his room, so that when the curtain was raised, the pillow would fall on the head of the person entering.

Bokuden first called his oldest son, who saw the pillow, took it down, entered the room, and replaced the pillow over the curtain.

As the second son entered, the pillow fell, but he caught it in his hands and placed it back over the curtain.

As the youngest son rushed in, the pillow fell squarely on his head, but he cut it in half with his sword before it hit the floor.

To the first son, Bokuden gave his sword, saying, "You are a great swordsman."

To the second son he said, "You will one day become a great swordsman, but you must yet train very hard."

To the third son he said, "You are a disgrace to this family, and are not qualified to even hold a sword." So saying, he took his youngest son's sword away from him and cast him out of the house.

—Traditional Story

Over the years, one question about self-defense has

been asked perhaps more than any other: "Sensei, what should I do if I get in my car, and someone hiding in the back seat grabs me by the throat or puts a gun to my head?" The correct answer has always been the same: "If a mugger is lurking in the back seat, don't get in the car." This is not a facetious answer. The plain fact is that there is little or nothing anyone can do when caught in a certain situation. In the case of the attack above, there are certain techniques which could be executed against the attacker, but their success would require a high degree of awareness of lapses in the attacker's attention. If one has such awareness, then he would surely be aware of the danger before entering the car.

People who master karate-do will be able to defend themselves in any situation, but not on the basis of physical ability only. The most important aspect of self-defense is for one to understand his position at all times and become aware enough of himself and his surroundings to be safe. Avoidance is always the best method of self-defense. But to avoid danger, one must be aware that the danger exists.

It is foolish to think that merely by training the body, one may be safe in any situation. Even the most skilled athlete cannot escape from a surprise attack if he is not aware of the attack until it hits. Once hit, the body may be too injured to respond. Therefore, the essence of karate self-defense must be awareness of the attack before it hits.

To more clearly understand this subject, one should consider types of attacks in two categories—surprise attack and contemplated attack. Contemplated attack is an attack which the defender perceives in advance, has time to think about, and responds to from a strong defensive position. The techniques and training of a first degree black belt are more than adequate to meet the challenge of almost any contemplated attack.

Surprise attack encompasses all types of attacks which are initiated before the defender is aware of them. Again, the skills of a first degree black belt are generally adequate to defend against many surprise attacks. The black belt will usually be able to nullify at least part of the force of an unarmed or armed attack due to his superior reflexes, timing and coordination. But these physical responses have their limits, and the parameters of those limits shrink with age. The goal to strive for is to relegate all potential attacks to the level of contemplated attacks. The method for doing this is the *Do* of karate-do.

First, we must train the body to make it strong; then we must train the mind. Awareness is not a quantitative "thing" which can be learned; it is a state of mind which must be realized. The ultimate goal is to maintain a feeling of concentration in the tanden twenty-four hours a day. Using the tanden as a focal point, we may then proceed to develop awareness of the environment.

Using the example of the mugger lurking in the back seat of a car, consider the value of training your mind to focus on the tanden every time you approach a car door. This is relatively easy to master. When you do your daily mokuso, place the image of the car in your mind. Visualize yourself walking toward the car, lowering your breathing to the tanden, and looking in the back seat. Visualize the back seat empty, and see yourself get in, calm and secure. Visualize an attacker in the back seat, and see yourself walking away calmly to call the police or seek shelter. It is not difficult. Then, when you actually walk to your car, do the same thing. You will find a keen sense of calmness and a general feeling of well-being. By concentrating on your breathing, you will feel no fear.

The aware mind is not paranoid. Paranoia is laden with fear, while the aware mind is devoid of fear. The simple exercise of looking in the back seat every time one enters a car will develop strength rather than fear. For we are not afraid that someone might be in the car; we are afraid that he might attack us if we get in and that we would be helpless. Therefore, we can overcome that fear completely by not getting in.

Martial artists often refer to this kind of thinking as "samurai strategy." The samurai warriors placed the highest priority on one's position in any situation and the strategic use of that position for self-defense. In the case of the car, we should think of our actions in terms of "position." Being outside the car when we perceive the danger is the best possible position to be in: we can run and avoid the confrontation altogether. Being inside the car when the danger is perceived is a very bad position. If you get in the car and then realize that you forgot to check the back seat, turn around immediately and look. That would put you in a better position for defense than if you were driving when you perceived the danger. This kind of thinking is essential in the development of awareness for self-defense.

To take another example, assume that you have just entered a room full of people, most of whom you do not know. This could be a PTA meeting, a cocktail party or even a theater. Someone you know calls out to you from the other side of the room and beckons you to come over.

You simply walk through the crowd to your friend. Such a reaction is very bad, for you are throwing away an opportunity to train your mind and heighten your awareness. Instead of mindlessly walking through the crowd, pause for a few seconds when you enter the room, and exercise your mind with samurai strategy. Drop your breathing to your tanden and first observe the approximate number of people in the room. Second, see where the exits are, and look at the windows to see if they could be used as exits. Third, observe whether people are in small groups or scattered. Fourth, consider the atmosphere: is there tension or joviality? What you are doing is determining your position in terms of self-defense. Samurai strategy is a diverting and pleasant game which helps develop a sense of well-being and increases your powers of observation.

If there is a large group of people between you and your friend, perhaps the best strategy would be to walk around the group rather than through it. Perhaps a small group is arguing and another is joking. It would be better to walk through the happy group, even if you have to walk farther. Perhaps no one calls to you. In this case, it might be better to take a position as close as possible to an exit. But be aware of what is outside the exit: an attack could come from that direction also.

If you sit down, think about the chair in terms of self-defense. Is it a stuffed chair in which you would sink down and be unable to rise from quickly? Does it have arms which could restrict your movements? If it has arms the same height as the table it is next to, don't pull it up to the table and box yourself in. Will the legs of the chair slide on the floor, or will they stick? Is it possible to sit with your back to the wall? If you sit on a sofa, it is better to sit on the end so that you may not be attacked from both sides at once.

Consider the manner in which you sit. If you bend far over and grasp the chair with both hands to pull it to you, you are vulnerable to attack. Bent over, looking down with both hands behind you is a poor position. Sit down straight, and maintain feeling in the tanden. Learn to sit and rise from center (hara).

Again, bear in mind that samurai strategy is a game, but it is a game which will become part of you and protect you from danger. As you exercise the strategy, forget about fear. Fear has no part in it. You are training your mind to be aware; you are not worrying about being attacked.

In its broadest manifestations, self-defense is not limited to personal defense against an assailant. In a larger sense, it is defense of the human organism against *all* threats. In this sense, self-defense includes the act of looking both ways before crossing the street. Through experience and training, we learn to be aware of the danger of crossing a street without looking. In a similar fashion, one does not slice a tomato by holding it with one hand and raising the other hand high over the head to quickly slash downward with a sharp knife. It is not that the tomato would not be cut; it is that we know better than to perform such a careless and dangerous act.

Practicing samurai strategy is merely a method for teaching us to be careful and prudent at all times.

It is most important that while playing the strategy game, you let no one know that you are doing it. It must be natural and private, so that it can become a part of you as you actually are, without pretense or affectation.

The goals of this exercise are similar to the goals of training a blind person. Blind people seem to hear better than the rest of us, but in fact they are simply more aware of sounds. Their perception of sound is heightened because they must rely on it for all their vital information. Samurai strategy is a method of heightening *all* perceptions, and making the person less vulnerable to attack.

The more you exercise your mind in this direction, the less chance you will have to fall victim to surprise attack.

Chapter 11

Karate-do and Zen Together—A Way of Life

Yasuoki was a great warrior who specialized in the use of the spear. Since he was also a shogun at a young age, he was full of pride. Nothing incensed him more than hearing about the presence of mind of the zen masters and how they could perceive an attack before it occurred.

To test the validity of the stories and to dispel what he felt were hateful rumors, he invited the great zen master, Bankei, to visit him.

While he and Bankei were chatting and sipping tea, Yasuoki suddenly grabbed his spear and thrust it violently at Bankei.

With seeming nonchalance, Bankei diverted the head of the spear with his rosary and said, "Tsk, tsk. Lousy technique. You're too excited."

Following this encounter, Yasuoki became the greatest spearsman in Japan, and he always said that Bankei was the sensei who taught him the most about his art.

—Traditional Story

The singular distinction of a pure martial art like karate-do is that its mastery bears direct applications to day-to-day living, personality, psychological stability and survival. We know that the connection between training in the dojo and conducting the business of day-to-day life lies in zen. But it is important that we do not separate the zen experience from our karate training, just as we should not separate our karate training from our daily lives. If lines are drawn between zen and karate and everyday living, all three disciplines suffer. Delimitations are alien to the spirit of zen and karate-do, and if we believe in the spirit of bushido, we also believe in the unity of all things in the cosmos. Therefore, it is instructive to consider the great precepts of zen in relation to karate-do and to scrutinize the possible impact of these precepts on our everyday lives.

In zen, we are encouraged to break our psychological attachments to "things" and especially to thinking and theorizing. In karate this is manifested in the strong emphasis placed on allowing the body to move freely through intuition. Thinking takes time, and time creates *suki*. A pause in kata appears as a jerky, unnatural movement. In sparring it appears as instant defeat. In everyday living, too much thinking about the potential consequences of a decision results in frustration and anxiety. Facing a difficult life decision should be viewed in the same light as facing a skilled opponent: let your mind mirror your opponent (problem), and strike forcefully from hara the instant you sense an opening.

Zen also concerns itself with the nature of death, and tells us to understand death and then forget it. In karate we perceive death as the fear to go forward, and we strive rigorously to prevent that fear from interfering with total committment in technique. Once we perceive death and pain as natural eventualities, we can throw them out of our conscious being and perform our techniques boldly.

When we have no thought for our own lives, we can become truly selfless in our relations with others. If we think about others, and not our own reward or penalty, we will act quickly, without hesitation or question.

Zen teaches us to let our minds move freely. In karate this is encouraged by being open-minded to our sensei, our seniors, our peers and our juniors. The student of karate must not become self-satisfied or rest on the laurels of his achievements. He must always try new techniques and seek new ideas and training methods. In the dojo and out, we can be efficient only if we relax and proceed from hara. Since a closed mind is a stiff mind, and a stiff mind cannot reside in a relaxed body, only those with open minds can completely relax.

By breaking our attachments to illusions through zen, we eliminate doubt and suspicion. This is basic to the idea of budo, which means "to stop conflict." In the dojo, the elimination of doubt and suspicion is supported by the demand for complete trust and faith in the wisdom and experience of the sensei. When we are suspicious of the motives or intentions of friends or business acquaintances, it is frequently because we have not eliminated the conflicts in our own thinking. Through trusting our partners in sparring, we learn that self-respect is the foundation of respect for others.

The calm mind strived for in zen is developed in karate training by learning to withhold one's inner feelings from the opponent. The stable emotions gained in sparring and self-defense can serve the student well in any stressful situation. Through training we can learn how to center our emotions to overcome anxiety. When we can overcome anxiety associated with direct attack, we will find day-to-day stresses to be far less problematic.

As zen teaches us to rely on our intuition, karate teaches us to concentrate on "feeling" rather than thinking. We are taught to develop our personal style from basic ideas and to understand the cyclical nature of the universe (*shu-ha-ri*). By carrying this concept into our daily lives, we will be less perplexed by changes in our bodies and lifestyles and environments. The master of karate-do tends to view happenings in a broader scope, and perceives relationships between seemingly disparate events. This reduces the natural, psychological resistance to change, and enables one to be more satisfied with the course and direction of his life.

The practice of zen results in increased sensitivity to the ebb and flow of the cosmos. Through sparring and self-defense, one develops great sensitivity to the feelings and intentions of the opponent; through kata, one develops sensitivity to one's own body and to the environment. The karate student also becomes more sensitive to the ebb and flow if ki, both in himself and in others. Heightened sensitivity to how others feel is very beneficial in the development of any personal relationship. Further, in sparring we give and receive with complete sincerity, and following the same rule in daily life results in greatly increased understanding of how others feel when they are giving and receiving.

One of the greatest contributions of zen to karate-do is the concept that what we see on the outside is a reflection of what is inside us. That is, fear of an opponent, for example, does not lie in the opponent, but only inside the one who is afraid. Thus, if one gains control over himself, he will gain control over the opponent. In this regard we may say that actions are the mirror of the mind. What a person *does* reveals more about him than what he says. At the same time, the mind is the mirror of actions. That is, those who are truly modest and sincere in their minds will act modest and sincere in their daily lives. Those who feel inferior will work the hardest to impress others.

From these basic connections, each person can begin to live by the precepts of his art, both in the dojo and out.

The fundamental precept of character change and development is the same in any area of endeavor—karate-do, Alcoholics Anonymous or psychotherapy. It is that the individual must *want* to grow and change. No amount of discipline or work or counselling will help anyone unless he *wants* it to help. As Jigoro Kano pointed out, the martial arts will improve an individual only if he consciously seeks to carry over the positive aspects of his training into his daily life.

In karate-do, as in everything else, we must accept and remember that what we get out of it is what we put into it. If we expect and seek improvement, we will obtain it; if we expect failure, we will fail before we even begin.

THE POSITIVE LIFESTYLE

Of all the Western "isms" conceived in the 20th century, none has had a more deeply felt and far ranging impact on men and women than "assertivism." That we have felt compelled to coin this new word to explain our past failures points irrevocably to our continuing failure to move out of our emotional defensiveness. If we accept the premise of the modern psychologists who espouse assertiveness as the ultimate cure for everything from cancer to psoriasis, then we must also accept that the majority of us are a dopey, dithering, ignorant lot who would not recognize common sense if we died of it. From Freud to Fromm and from Esalen to est, we are bombarded with propaganda which says, in effect, "You have a problem. You can solve it by getting to know yourself better. Come to us, and we will teach you how." What this really is saying to us is that we, alone as individuals, are so ignorant that we can't even recognize our own problems, much less begin to solve them without a doctor or therapist or guru. While it is true that people often need outside help, it is the premise of karate-do, as set forth here, that anyone (barring psychosis) is more than adequately equipped to recognize his own strengths and liabilities, and to be as happy and emotionally stable as he chooses to be. All one needs is the desire to move forward.

The *Do* of karate-do cherishes and nourishes one great truth above all else: It is better to be positive than negative. This message of karate-do has had limited impact in America because of one great failing: it has been introduced by the Japanese as a macho activity, limited in scope to those men who must be tough, ultra-masculine and brave. Perhaps this approach could work in America if karate required a handgun in application. But since the techniques require a lifetime of hard work, karate-do has been relegated to the realm of the exotic, the eccentric and the eclectic. Indeed, the admixture of karate and native American commercialism has often crossed the threshhold of the bizzare. Impressed as we are by it, how many of us would actually want to appear half-naked on national television and have a watermelon sliced on our stomach by an Oriental in carnival attire? That is not karate-do; it is not even karate-jitsu. Considering that a watermelon will split by itself when cut to a depth of three inches or so, it is not even a good show. Irrespective of the ludicrous theatrics, such demonstrations foster the impression that people who seriously study karate-do are all like the person holding the watermelon or the one holding the sword.

Since this crude commercialism shows no signs of abating, it is unlikely that in the near future karate-do will be considered seriously by very many people in America. Nevertheless, it is incumbent on Americans who have some sense of the truth to spread that truth as far and wide as possible. When the old masters passed along their art to others, they did not do it for reasons of commercialism or profit. Virtually none of them was ever paid for teaching. Rather, they taught their art as an artist teaches a protege. The art is passed on because it is a valuable and beneficial thing for people to have. Modern society, of course, operates on money. But far more important than making money and supporting a fancy dojo is the importance of living the spirit of karate-do on a daily basis. If the art will help people to live more peaceably, to gain good health, and to think more clearly, its propagation will be justified. If, on the other hand, it becomes a sport or a sideshow and contributes to frustrated masculinity and femininity, it should die, and probably will.

Idealism aside, the art of karate-do bears very important benefits for modern man.

First, it teaches us to distinguish between assertiveness and aggressiveness. Assertiveness is a matter of moving out of emotional defensiveness and expressing oneself in a clear, positive fashion, both in words and actions. Aggressiveness is over-compensation for insecurity, and it manifests itself in a person who forces his ideas and actions on another in a rude and obnoxious manner. Distinguishing between aggressiveness and assertiveness in someone is simple: if we don't like someone's attitude, he is aggresive (or, as some modern psychologists insist on saying, "over-aggressive"). But in our own selves, in the deepest recesses of our minds, we often fail to make the proper distinction. What is lurking there as our honest feeling or opinion is kept there, subdued, usually because we do not want to hurt someone's feelings. Instead, we tend to take the indirect or flatly dishonest approach. Thus when a friend asks, "Don't you *love* my new dress?", we say, "Oh, it's really lovely," when in fact we think it is ugly and garish. Karate-do teaches us to go forward boldly and to be honest and direct. At the same time it teaches us to practice courtesy. So instead of saying to our friend, "No, I think your dress is horribly ugly," we might take the first step toward seeking the truth of the matter and being courteous at the same time. For example, we might say, "It really fits you well!" Although this example is simplistic, it is a very real exercise in moving forward toward becoming a positive individual.

On a larger scale, the development of a positive or negative personality is precipitated by how much of our attention we award to various kinds of behavior. In the dojo, for example, we learn to be aware of even the smallest movements of our opponent. But we learn to distinguish between movements which are designed to distract us and movements which are designed to destroy us. To do this effectively, we must become aware of the intention of the other party. If we once respond to a feint or an extranneous movement of an opponent during sparring, we forever will be controlled by that opponent; he will repeat that movement as often as we foolishly respond to it. As art mirrors life, we learn from our training that people act toward us in a certain fashion because of the way we respond to their actions. When a husband shouts at his wife and aggressively dominates her, he does so because her response encourages him to do it. Perhaps he knows that his hatefulness is painful to her, and that she cries privately in remorse. Her awarding of so much attention—so much crying and depression—to his foul manner is precisely the reason he continues his aggressiveness. Her response fulfills his basic human desire to be "in control." It is no secret that a person who feels out of control of his own emotions can often derive great satisfaction from being in control of someone else's emotions. While we cannot hope to change the overall attitude of such a person, we certainly can let him know by our assertive response that *we* will not be controlled or intimidated. Just as we do not award our attention to superfluous movements of the opponent in sparring, we can alter a domineering person's attitude toward us by saying, "If you feel that way and want to act that way, it is your business. But I have no time or interest to waste worrying about it. You may continue to rant and rave as much as you like, but it won't affect me." In effect, we are telling the other person that we do not care enough about his particular actions to be bothered by them. We are also removing the essential element of any conflict—the opposition. If there is no opponent, there is no conflict.

From karate-do we learn to be direct without being caustic, as in sparring forcefully, but with control. We learn to be aware of the feelings and intentions of the other person, and to determine whether he is angry, confused, or simply as direct as we are. We learn that fear of an opponent is just like emotional defensiveness, and we work hard to overcome it. When we coach others, we learn to express our ideas clearly, directly, and without digressions or repetitions.

Perhaps the greatest service paid to the person who diligently pursues his art from a high point of view is the ability to focus on the other person. This implies a great deal. It implies that in this fast-paced, highly opinionated society, the sincere karate-ka can calmly and sincerely listen to what the other person is saying. By daily relating to all kinds of people in the dojo as peers, he can actually learn to acknowledge the value of another person's thoughts and ideas. Regardless of the type of individual he encounters in the dojo, he learns to form a bridge from his own thoughts to the thoughts of the other person. He finds that, regardless of background or attitude or race or personality, everyone in the dojo is striving toward the same goals. If he works very hard at it, he can perceive the essence of all conflicts between people as a matter of inflexible pride and aggressive ego. He learns that people can exist peaceably together without agreeing on every detail. As he moves deeper into his art and starts teaching others, he learns to be assertive in a positive fashion, without being aggressive or domineering.

When we can put aside our own thoughts and emotions

and ego and pride, we can actively listen to what the other person is saying. The result of focusing on the other person is called self-confidence. If we are confident of our own ability to think and to reason and to act when necessary, we will be able to relate to other people without fear of rejection, without frustration, and without feelings of inferiority.

The entire process of character change and development in karate-do rests, for better or worse, entirely on the desire of the individual to recognize and use it. In the dojo there is no psychologist, no therapist and no guru. A good sensei is the embodiment of the literal translation of his title: "One who has gone before." If he is sincere, he will push his students to their limits and beyond. He will point the way to the correct path, but he will not interfere with the student's right to be what he chooses to be. If the student is sincere, he will follow his sensei and consciously seek to find the truth.

This is the path of enlightenment; this is the path of karate-do.

Chapter 12

Meeting Myself

Among karate people, there exists an unwritten code which dictates that we swap stories of seemingly inhuman feats performed by our instructors. Not only are these stories interesting, but they also bestow on the storyteller a sense of self-importance, as if by telling the story one obtains some of the skill of the masters. I have been as faithful to this code as anyone, and I certainly have witnessed feats which stir the imagination.

I have faced the great masters in free-sparring: Hirokazu Kanazawa, Keinosuke Enoeda, Taiji Kase, Takayuki Mikami. I tell grand tales of Kanazawa standing fifteen feet away and punching me before I could raise my arm to block; of Enoeda sweeping both my legs from beneath me, from behind (I never saw him move); of Mikami flinging me about the dojo like a yo-yo; and of Kase literally running over me as if I did not exist. My favorite, perhaps, is the tale of Hidetaka Nishiyama, the greatest of the great JKA karate masters, beckoning me to demonstrate sparring with him in front of the local television cameras. My whole life flashed before me as he executed a blindingly fast front thrust kick to my chin, stopping me in mid-charge. He held his foot there just long enough for my mind to register the impression of his toes against my lower lip. It was at that instant I decided that, given a choice, I would much rather be shot with a

.38 pistol than hit by Nishiyama-sensei's foot or hand. Bullets, after all, leave the victim some chance of survival.

As exciting as my tales of wonder are, they really are pointless. I know they are pointless because some of my students now tell semi-fantastic tales about my exploits, and I have never done anything fantastic. I am still a beginner.

I would enjoy writing down all my fantastic tales for posterity, but that would deprive me of regaling my peers and embelishing the tales as necessary. What I will record here are stories of fact without embellishment. They flow through my subconscious like wind through a bamboo grove. They taught me then, and they re-teach me everytime they appear.

STARTING OVER

I knew it was going to be a bad day as soon as I bowed. "No! Start over!", Sensei barked. *Start over?*, I thought. *All I did was bow!*

Hidetaka Nishiyama, the great master, had come two thousand miles to see my students for the first time. I was surprised that, in front of my students, Nishiyama-sensei treated me with great deference, as if I were a peer. For the first two days he buttressed my confidence, talked intimately with me, and stroked my ego. By the second day I was riding high on a wave of thick pride.

It was now the third and final day of his visit, and he announced that we would each perform our favorite kata under his attentive and critical eye. "You first," he said, pointing at me. "Everyone warm up."

Since I badly lacked regular instruction, I asked him if

I could perform my weakest kata, the kata about which I had the most questions. "Fine," he said; "Good idea."

And now I was standing on the floor in front of him, with all my students' eyes trained on me. I was ready to give them a show—to show them the excellence of my techniques. Then they would know why I had risen to a position of such high esteem in the eyes of the great Sensei.

"Start over!" he barked again. "You have no *zanshin*! Where is your spirit?"

My first thought was one of embarrassment. Oh, well. My students probably wouldn't even remember such a minor error. But after bowing the fifth time, I forgot about my students. I even forgot about the whir of the movie camera recording the fiasco. All I could hear was Nishiyama's harsh scolding. He and I were the only two people in existence, and my only desire was to perform the first movement of the kata.

"Hai! First movement! One!" he shouted.

Grateful for my release from torture, I performed that movement as it had never been performed before—smooth, graceful, flowing, strong, full of feeling and intensity.

"Oh, oh, oh," He shook his head sadly. "No," he said, adjusting my head. "No," he said, adjusting my arms. "No, no, no." He continued with my shoulders, my back, my legs, my knees, my feet, and my toes. Finally, he kicked my rump and whacked my belly, hard.

"Start over!"

And so it went, over and over, again and again, through each movement of the kata: me performing the movement endlessly, Nishiyama whacking, smacking, thumping, scolding. And always the same admonition, "Start over!" For forty-five minutes we continued. No rest. *I'm going to pass out*, I thought. "Start over!" *I can't breathe*! "Start over!" *I can't see him. Where did he go*? "Start over!" Suddenly I knew it. I knew it as well as I knew my own name: If he said "start over" just one more time, I would expire. I was going to die, and I didn't care.

"Hai! Finished! Bow!" His voice came as gentle rain on parched desert. It was over.

As I turned, I saw the awed faces of my students staring at me, mouths agape. They will probably all quit, I thought, now that they have seen how lousy I really am.

Then Nishiyama patted me gently on the back, smiled, and very quietly so no one else could hear, said, "Very good kata."

"Next!"

A TRUE MASTER

In the course of karate training, one has good days and bad days. Especially at the beginning and intermediate levels, when students are still trying to impress their peers, it seems like one person's voice rises above the din of the locker room after training. It is the voice of the lucky guy who had an exceptionally good day and was rewarded with the Sensei's attention. His moment in the sun is always fleeting, and he generally takes advantage of it quickly and loudly. It is an exercise in pure egotism.

Such moments are rare for me, so I was doubly pleased when my chance came one hot, July day. I was preparing to test for the black belt, and my spirit was very high. Disregarding the humid, one hundred and four degree midwestern heat, Sensei pushed us hard for more than two hours. The class began with hundreds of kicks and punches, followed by intense semi-free sparring with the emphasis on a new and difficult shifting maneuver. It seemed that everyone was struggling and stumbling—everyone but me. I was performing as if I had invented all of it. Even after spirit training—one thousand kicks, one hundred sit-ups, two hundred punches on the makiwara, fifteen laps around the dojo—I felt fresh and enerjetic. During free sparring with my sempai, I reached the zenith of all my achievements: I scored two half-points on him, and he didn't even retaliate.

What a joy it was to strut into the locker room while others dragged! My best friend, a student of equal rank, slumped on the bench in a sweating stupor while I bounced around the room, expounding, bragging, and explaining the details of techniques to all present, whether they wanted to hear it or not. My friend slumped, expressionless, and said nothing. For five or ten minutes I continued. Still jabbering, I yanked off my belt and jacket, dropping my towel on the floor. As I stooped to retrieve it, I cracked my forehead hard on a protruding clothes hook. Stunned, I bounced backward onto the bench a few feet from my friend. Dazed, I sat motionless for several minutes. Gradually I became aware of blood trickling from my forehead and running down to my chin. Slowly I turned toward my friend.

Still expressionless, he sighed, "Yeah. A true master."

A Nail Sticking Up

Among karate instructors, a common axiom is, "If a

nail sticks up, knock it down." This phrase is put to use frequently in the dojo, and is a simplistic suggestion on how to handle inflated egos and braggadocio. While still a brown belt, I learned that the implementation of this axiom can take many forms.

For as long as I can remember, I have loved to talk. I started talking when I was nine months old, and against the wishes of many, I have never stopped. This has served me well in many areas of my life. I have frequently escaped the role of a fool by talking rapidly and confidently, as if I knew what I was talking about. That is what I was doing in the dojo one day when Sensei caught me. He overheard me expounding in the locker room, and said, simply, "Enough talk, Let's go."

Throughout the class session, he paid little attention to me as I continuously corrected one of the newer members. Then, toward the end of the class, he beckoned me to the front of the room to help him demonstrate a point. I would attack while he defended and made explanations. Suddenly he stopped, and almost as an afterthought asked me, loudly, "Mr. Hassell, do you like girls?"

"Uh, well, yes, Sensei, I do."

"Do you have a girlfriend?"

"A girlfriend?" I asked, thoroughly bewildered.

"Yes, Mr. Hassell. I'm speaking English. A *girlfriend*."

This is a test, I thought. *Speak crisply to your sensei.* "Yes, Sensei!" I shouted.

"Do you ever arm wrestle with her?"

"Do I what?"

"Mr. Hassell!"

"No, Sensei! I never arm wrestle with my girlfriend!"

"Good!" he shouted. "You are so weak, she would beat you! You are the most terriblest brown belt I ever see!"

"Thank you, Sensei!"

"You are welcome. Get back in line."

To this day, I listen closely and speak very little when my seniors are present.

Now I Know

In good karate dojos today, people do not get beat up or grossly humiliated, and they are never in fear of losing their lives. But among some of the Japanese instructors in the 1960's, the actions which today would result in lawsuits, were then merely everyday training methods. Some of the Japanese instructors had not yet reconciled themselves to the fact that America is a land of team sports and that Americans, by and large, will not accept severe, individual torture, no matter how worthy the cause. Consequently, many talented people were driven away from karate. Some of us, however, had begun training at a very early age, and we simply did not know that most people would not submit themselves to the kind of pressure we took for granted. And it was from that severe, individual pressure that we gained some of our deepest insights.

I clearly remember the instant I began to understand the essence of karate-do. As was my custom, I had driven two hundred and fifty miles to spend the weekend training with the only Japanese instructor for the JKA in the midwest. I was an eighteen year old brown belt at the time, and my ego was in full bloom.

We would arrive at the dojo around midnight each Friday, and would begin training at 10:00 a.m. Saturday. Saturday training always continued until four or five o'clock in the afternoon, and we generally spent the evening visiting other dojos. One dojo regularly showed Japanese films until midnight on Saturday. When we watched these samurai movies, we would get inspired and go back to our dojo to practice. Since we had no money, Sensei would let us sleep in the dojo on the bare wood floor. Invariably, we were so exhausted by two or three a.m., that the hard floor was no inconvenience at all. And our youthful vigor made it easy for us to rise for five or six more hours of training on Sunday morning.

But on this particular Saturday night, Sensei walked into the dojo at 3:30 a.m. and loudly instructed us to get up and practice our kata.

Although thoroughly bewildered, we obediently got up, put on our trousers, and started practicing while Sensei beat the makiwara into oblivion. There were only two of us, and we kept giving each other questioning looks. *What is this all about?* we wondered.

After a half hour or so, Sensei told us to face each other for free sparring. We had been fighting lightly for a few minutes when he stopped us and said to me, "You don't know how to block. Anyone could punch you in the face. The only feeling you have for your face is fear." He then had me stand in natural stance while my friend performed lunge punches toward my face. Again and again he punched, and each time I shifted and executed a rising block. *Basic sparring?* I thought. *This is silly. How can I show him my strength if he won't let me fight?*

Gradually, my left arm became heavy. I was tired, and

my forearm ached. "No! Same arm!" Sensei barked, as I shifted to block with my other arm. "Now, harder! Faster! Stronger!" he yelled at my friend. Soon I was breathing very hard. Sweat blinded me, and the whole left side of my body felt as if it were being hit by a sledgehammer. Harder and harder my friend punched, until I was sure I was going to cry. Finally, I staggered backwards and literally begged, "Sensei, *please* tell me what I am doing wrong!"

Shaking his head in disgust, he turned to my friend. "This fella wears a brown belt and acts like a baby. Punch harder! If he doesn't block, hit him! Now!"

This time I moved fast, but my arm was just too tired, and I ducked, desperately trying to avoid the inevitable. BANG! I thought for an instant that someone had slammed a door. But then the pain exploded in my head, and I knew my left eye was black. It was tearing. In fact, both eyes were tearing. Against my will, I was crying.

"Sensei, what am I doing wrong?!"

"Quiet! Hit him again!"

BANG! This time it was my upper lip. I was bleeding.

"Sensei . . .!"

"Again!"

BANG! My nose was bleeding. I literally ran backwards, crying, "Sensei, please tell me what I'm doing wrong!" My whole body felt like it was on fire, and I was terrified. I really wanted to die.

With inhuman speed, Sensei charged up to me, his nose almost touching mine, and screamed, "IF I TELL YOU, YOU WON'T KNOW!" He stayed there for what seemed like hours, his glaring eyes burning into mine. It seemed like time stopped.

After several minutes, he turned and walked back to his original position. My tears were gone, and I felt no pain. In complete silence, I walked back to my friend and bowed. He punched, and I blocked, perfectly. After several more minutes of silent observation, Sensei bowed and left the dojo.